Name _____ Class _____ Date _____

Skills Worksheet

Concept Review

Section: Atomic Nuclei and Nuclear Stability

Answer the following questions in the space provided.

1. What is a nucleon?

_____

_____

2. What is a nuclide?

_____

_____

3. Describe how the strong force attracts nucleons.

_____

_____

_____

_____

4. What is nuclear binding energy?

_____

_____

_____

_____

5. How is nuclear binding energy related to the mass defect?

_____

_____

_____

_____

_____

| Concept Review *continued*

In the blanks at the left, write the letter of the choice that best completes the statement or answers the question.

_____ **6.** What is another name for the nucleus of an atom?
      a. isotope
      b. mass number
      c. nucleon
      d. nuclide

_____ **7.** These are atoms that have the same atomic number but different mass numbers.
      a. isotopes
      b. nuclei
      c. nucleons
      d. nuclides

_____ **8.** Which of the following does NOT represent an isotope of tellurium?
      a. $^{122}_{52}\text{Te}$
      b. $^{124}_{52}\text{Te}$
      c. $^{128}_{52}\text{Te}$
      d. $^{124}_{53}\text{Te}$

_____ **9.** What is the force of attraction among the particles in a nucleus that overcomes electrostatic repulsion and holds the nucleus together?
      a. electrostatic force
      b. strong force
      c. electromagnetic force
      d. nuclear binding force

_____ **10.** Which of the following does not occur when separated nucleons come together to form a nucleus?
      a. the release of energy
      b. instability of the nucleus
      c. increased stability of the nucleus
      d. a mass defect

Name _____ Class _____ Date _____

Complete each statement below by choosing a term from the following list. You will not use every term.

decrease	per nucleon	less	large	mole
nucleus	maximum	highest	separate	stable
protons	mass	$^{24}_{12}Mg$	repulsions	mass number
increase	mass defect	attraction	$^{56}_{26}Fe$	nuclear binding

11. The _____ represents the amount of _____ converted

into energy and released when a _____ is formed from protons and

neutrons. Specifically, if one _____ of $^{16}_{8}O$ nuclei were to be formed

from 8 mol of protons and 8 mol of neutrons, the resulting 1 mol of nuclei

would have a mass that is 0.137005 g _____ than that of the original

_____ and neutrons. Stated differently, the _____

energy for $^{16}_{8}O$ is the amount of energy required to _____ 1 mol of

$^{16}_{8}O$ nuclei into 8 mol of protons and 8 mol of neutrons.

12. Consider a graph that plots average binding energy per nucleon versus mass

number. This graph shows that nuclear binding energies _____

rapidly with increasing mass number, reach a _____ around mass

number 55, and then slowly _____. The nuclei with the

_____ binding energies (mass numbers 40 to 150) are the most

stable. Beyond these elements, the nucleus is too _____ for added

nucleons to increase the overall _____ among the particles, and

_____ become more significant. Stated differently, isotopes that

have a high binding energy per nucleon are more _____. The most

stable nucleus is _____.

| Concept Review *continued*

Complete each statement below by writing the correct term in the space provided.

13. Because a strong force of attraction holds nuclear particles together, a

nucleus is at a _____ energy state than are its separated nucleons.

14. The energy produced during the formation of a nucleus is very

_____ compared with the energy changes that take place in ordi-
nary chemical reactions.

15. During the formation of a nucleus, energy is produced at the expense of

_____

Refer to the rules for predicting nuclear stability. Complete each statement by underlining the correct word in brackets.

16. All 256 of the known stable nuclei, represented by red dots, form a pattern
called the band of [stability, nuclear bonding].

17. Above atomic number 20, the most stable nuclides have [more, fewer] neutrons than protons.

18. Except for the smallest nuclei, all stable nuclei contain a number of neutrons
that is [less than or equal to, equal to or greater] than the number of protons.

19. Almost [60%, 90%] of all stable nuclei have even numbers of protons and
neutrons.

20. Nuclei with even numbers of protons and neutrons (an even-even combination) are particularly [unstable, stable].

21. $^{16}_{8}O$, $^{40}_{20}Ca$, and $^{88}_{38}Sr$ are nuclei with so-called magic numbers of nucleons and
tend to be very [unstable, stable].

Name _____ Class _____ Date _____

Concept Review

Section: Nuclear Change

Answer the following questions in the space provided.

1. What is radioactivity?

_____

_____

2. Describe what happens when a nucleus is stabilized by converting neutrons into protons.

_____

_____

_____

3. Describe what happens when a nucleus is stabilized by converting protons into neutrons.

_____

_____

_____

4. Describe what happens when a nucleus is stabilized by emitting positrons.

_____

_____

_____

5. Describe what happens when a nucleus is stabilized by losing alpha particles.

_____

_____

_____

Concept Review *continued*

6. Complete the following table about different types of radioactive decay.

Type of Radioactive Decay	What happens to the atomic number?	What happens to the mass number?
Beta-particle emission		
electron capture		
positron emission		
alpha particle emission		

Write balanced nuclear equations for the following, and name the type of radioactive emission formed when each occurs.

7. $^{51}_{24}Cr + ^{0}_{-1}e \rightarrow$ _____ $+ \gamma$ emission: _____

8. $^{226}_{88}Ra \rightarrow$ _____ $+ ^{4}_{2}He$ emission: _____

9. $^{239}_{93}Np \rightarrow$ _____ $+ ^{0}_{+1}e$ emission: _____

10. $^{234}_{91}Pa \rightarrow$ _____ $+ ^{0}_{-1}e$ emission: _____

11. $^{49}_{24}Cr \rightarrow ^{49}_{23}V +$ _____ emission: _____

12. $^{238}_{92}U \rightarrow ^{234}_{90}Th +$ _____ emission: _____

13. $^{214}_{83}Bi \rightarrow ^{214}_{84}Po +$ _____ emission: _____

Categorize each nuclear equation below by writing the correct term from the following list. Terms may be used more than once.

beta particle emission electron capture positron emission

alpha particle emission annihilation of matter

14. $^{0}_{-1}e + ^{0}_{+1}e \rightarrow 2\gamma$ type: _____

15. $^{1}_{1}p \rightarrow ^{1}_{0}n + ^{0}_{+1}e$ type: _____

16. $^{37}_{18}Ar + ^{0}_{-1}e \rightarrow ^{37}_{17}Cl + \gamma$ type: _____

17. $^{238}_{92}U \rightarrow ^{234}_{90}Th + ^{4}_{2}He$ type: _____

18. $^{1}_{0}n \rightarrow ^{1}_{1}H + ^{0}_{-1}e$ type: _____

| Concept Review *continued*

Complete each statement below by writing the correct term in the space provided.

19. Nuclei that have an excess of neutrons can become stable by emitting

_____.

20. Any time a particle collides with an _____, all of the mass of the two particles is converted into electromagnetic energy.

21. A positron colliding with an electron results in the conversion of all the

masses of the two particles into gamma rays; this process is known as the

_____.

22. _____ emission changes neither the atomic number nor the mass number.

23. In _____, a proton is changed into a neutron.

24. In beta emission, an electron is emitted by a _____.

25. None of the elements above atomic number 83 and mass number 126 have

stable isotopes, and many stabilize by _____.

26. A few sheets of paper can stop _____.

27. In an alpha emission, the atomic number of the nucleus decreases by

_____ while the mass number decreases by _____.

Complete each statement below by choosing a term from the following list. Use each term only once.

| fission | fusion | sustains | chain reaction | fuse |
| neutrons | binding energy | spontaneous | critical mass | |

28. Nuclear _____ refers to a nuclear reaction in which a very heavy

nucleus splits into two smaller nuclei, each having a higher _____

per nucleon than the original nucleus. A very small fraction of naturally

occurring uranium atoms undergoes _____ fission. Most fission

reactions are artificially induced by bombarding nuclei with _____.

A _____ is a fission reaction which, once initiated,

_____ itself. The smallest mass of radioactive material needed to

sustain a chain reaction is known as the _____ of the material.

| Concept Review *continued*

29. Nuclear _____ occurs when two small nuclei combine, or

_____, to form a larger, more stable nucleus with a higher binding

energy.

Categorize each nuclear equation below as *fission* or *fusion*.

30. $^{3}_{1}H + ^{2}_{1}H \rightarrow ^{4}_{2}He + ^{1}_{0}n$ type: _____

31. $^{239}_{94}Pu + ^{1}_{0}n \rightarrow ^{90}_{38}Sr + ^{147}_{56}Ba + 3^{1}_{0}n$ type: _____

32. $^{235}_{92}U \rightarrow ^{90}_{38}Sr + ^{144}_{58}Ce + ^{1}_{0}n + 4^{0}_{-1}e$ type: _____

33. $2^{3}_{2}He \rightarrow ^{4}_{2}He + 2^{1}_{1}H$ type: _____

Answer the following items in the space provided.

34. Describe potential benefits and hazards of nuclear fission.

_____

_____

_____

_____

_____

_____

_____

_____

| Concept Review *continued*

35. Describe nuclear fusion and its potential as an energy source.

_____

_____

_____

_____

_____

_____

_____

_____

_____

Skills Worksheet

Concept Review

Section: Uses of Nuclear Chemistry

Answer the following in the space provided.

1. Define half-life.

_____

_____

_____

_____

2. How can half-lives be used to determine an object's age?

_____

_____

_____

_____

_____

In the blanks at the left, write the letter of the choice that best completes the statement or answers the question.

_____ **3.** The equation $^{40}_{19}K + ^{0}_{-1}e \rightarrow ^{40}_{18}Ar + \gamma$ represents the decay of potassium-40 by _____ to argon-40.
   a. beta emission
   b. electron capture
   c. positron emission
   d. alpha decay

_____ **4.** Potassium-40, with a half-life of _____ years, is useful in dating ancient rocks and minerals.
   a. 1.28 million
   b. 1.28 trillion
   c. 12.8 billion
   d. 1.28 billion

_____ **5.** The equation $^{14}_{6}C \rightarrow ^{14}_{7}N + ^{0}_{-1}e$ represents the decay of carbon-14 by
_____ to nitrogen-14.
  a. beta emission
  b. electron capture
  c. positron emission
  d. alpha decay

_____ **6.** Carbon-14, useful in dating the plants and animals of Earth's food
chain, has a half-life of how many years?
  a. 5715
  b. 571.5
  c. 57 150
  d. None of the above

_____ **7.** If an original sample of carbon-14 has a mass of 10 g, at the end of
11 430 years, the amount of carbon-14 remaining would be _____ g.
  a. 2.5
  b. 5
  c. 10
  d. 50

_____ **8.** Smoke detectors rely on _____ to ionize gas molecules, which help to
detect smoky air.
  a. alpha particles
  b. beta particles
  c. positrons
  d. gamma rays

_____ **9.** The radioactive isotope used most widely in nuclear medicine is _____.
  a. thallium-201
  b. technetium-99
  c. americium-241
  d. radon-222

_____**10.** During a PET scan, gamma rays are detected by a scanner, which con-
verts the information into _____.
  a. a three-dimensional picture of a person's organs
  b. an image of a person's heart
  c. a photographic image of bone repair
  d. None of the above

| Concept Review *continued*

_____**11.** The identification of elements by which of the following has been put
to use in detecting art forgeries?
a. carbon-14 dating
b. radon-222 dating
c. neutron activation analysis
d. potassium-40 dating

_____**12.** People who work with radioactive isotopes are advised to limit their
exposure to how many rems per year?
a. 10
b. 5
c. 25
d. 2.5

_____**13.** A marked decrease in white-blood-cell count can result from a dose of
how many rems of radiation?
a. 0–25
b. 25–50
c. 50–100
d. more than 100

Answer the following in the space provided.

14. Compare acute and chronic exposure to radiation.

_____

_____

_____

_____

_____

15. What similarities do you notice about the nuclear reactions used in medicine
that are mentioned in the text?

_____

_____

_____

_____

_____

_____

Name _____ Class _____ Date _____

Solve the following problem, and write your answer in the spaces in the table.

16. The half-life of radon-222 is approximately 4 days. If a tube containing 1.00 microgram of radon were stored in a hospital clinic for 12 days, how much radon would remain in the tube? Use the table below to determine successive half-life amounts during the 12-day period.

Days	0	4	8	12
Radon remaining				

Solve the following problems, and write your answer in the space provided.

17. The half-life of iodine-131 is approximately 8 days. How much of an original sample will be left after 24 days?

18. Thorium-234 has a half-life of 24 days. If 1 gram remains in a sealed container after 72 days, how much was there to begin with?

19. You find an ancient artifact with a ratio of carbon-14 to carbon-12 that is one quarter the ratio in a similar object today. About how old is the artifact?

20. The half-life of polonium-218 is 3.0 minutes. What percentage of the original sample remains after 4 half-lives?

Name _____ Class _____ Date _____

Section: Atomic Nuclei and Nuclear Stability

In the space provided, write the letter of the term or phrase that best answers the question.

_____ **1.** What does the 96 in $^{244}_{96}$Cm in represent?
  a. mass number
  b. atomic number
  c. number of nucleons
  d. number of neutrons

_____ **2.** What does the 254 in fermium-254 represent?
  a. mass number
  b. atomic number
  c. number of neutrons
  d. number of protons

_____ **3.** Isotopes of an element have the same
  a. mass number.
  b. atomic number.
  c. number of nucleons.
  d. number of neutrons.

_____ **4.** The strong force
  a. acts over a distance much larger than the electrostatic repulsion.
  b. accounts for attraction and repulsion between two nucleons.
  c. is stronger than the electrostatic repulsion.
  d. All of the above

_____ **5.** Nucleons are made of fundamental particles called
  a. neutrons.
  b. positrons.
  c. protons.
  d. quarks.

_____ **6.** The interaction that binds nucleons together in a nucleus describes
  a. binding energy.
  b. fission.
  c. radioactivity.
  d. the strong force.

Quiz *continued*

_____ **7.** The mass defect of a nuclide can be calculated by
   a. $A - (Z + N)$.
   b. (total mass of separate nucleons) − mass of nuclide.
   c. mass of protons − mass neutrons.
   d. $\dfrac{N}{Z}$.

_____ **8.** Assuming the speed of light is 3×10^8 m/s, the binding energy of a
   nuclide that has a mass defect of 10^{-30} kg is about
   a. 10^{-30} J.
   b. 10^{-23} J.
   c. 10^{-14} J.
   d. 10^8 J.

_____ **9.** Disregarding hydrogen and helium, as the mass number of a nuclide
   increases, the binding energy per nucleon
   a. falls sharply.
   b. remains constant.
   c. rises and then gradually falls.
   d. varies unpredictably.

_____ **10.** Which of the following general statements would account for instability
   of the nuclide $^{214}_{82}$ Pb?
   a. Except for $^1_1$H and $^3_2$He, a stable nucleus has N equal to or greater
      than Z.
   b. A stable nucleus has an $\dfrac{N}{Z}$ value between 1 and 1.5.
   c. A stable nucleus has the number of protons equaling an even num-
      ber and the number of neutrons equaling an even number.
   d. All nuclides that have atomic number greater than 83 and a mass
      number greater than 209 are unstable.

Name _____ Class _____ Date _____

Quiz

Section: Nuclear Change

In the space provided, write the letter of the term or phrase that best answers the question.

_____ **1.** The process $_0^1n \rightarrow {}_{+1}^{1}p + {}_{-1}^{0}e$ represents a(n)
   a. alpha-decay
   b. beta-decay
   c. electron capture
   d. fusion

_____ **2.** The nuclear reaction $_{11}^{21}\text{Na} \rightarrow {}_{10}^{21}\text{Ne} + {}_{+1}^{0}e$ occurs through the process of
   a. annihilation.
   b. positron emission
   c. electron capture
   d. fission

_____ **3.** A nuclide that undergoes alpha decay has its atomic number
   a. increased by 2.
   b. increased by 4.
   c. decreased by 2.
   d. decreased by 4.

_____ **4.** Which pair of particles can undergo the process of annihilation together?
   a. $_0^1n$, $_0^1n$
   b. $_{+1}^{1}p$, $_1^1\text{H}$
   c. $_{+1}^{1}p$, $_{-1}^{0}e$
   d. $_{+1}^{0}e$, $_{-1}^{0}e$

_____ **5.** Which of the particles balances the equation for the following nuclear reaction? $_3^7\text{Li} + \_\_\_\_ \rightarrow {}_2^4\text{He} + {}_2^4\text{He}$.
   a. $_2^4\text{He}$
   b. $_0^1n$
   c. $_1^1\text{H}$
   d. $_{-1}^{0}e$

Quiz *continued*

_____ **6.** Which of the following statements is true about nuclear fission?
   a. Fission occurs most often naturally.
   b. Fission produces nuclei that are each more massive than the original nuclei.
   c. Fission produces nuclei that are more stable than the original nuclei.
   d. Fission is the primary process that produces energy in stars.

_____ **7.** Which of the following characteristics describes a nuclear chain reaction?
   a. The process is used to sustain a fission reaction.
   b. The particle that starts the reaction is also produced by the reaction.
   c. It is uncontrollable.
   d. Both (a) and (b)

_____ **8.** Which of the following items adjust the rate of the chain reactions in a nuclear reactor?
   a. control rods
   b. coolant
   c. moderator
   d. uranium fuel rods

_____ **9.** The nuclear waste from a nuclear reactor is
   a. a useful source of heat.
   b. made up mostly of uranium-235.
   c. often released to the environment.
   d. radioactive and harmful.

_____ **10.** The nuclear reaction $4\ {}^{1}_{1}\text{H} \rightarrow {}^{4}_{2}\text{He} + 2\ {}^{0}_{+1}e$ is an example of
   a. a plasma.
   b. fission.
   c. fusion.
   d. radioactive decay.

Assessment

Quiz

Section: Uses of Nuclear Chemistry

In the space provided, write the letter of the term or phrase that best answers the question.

Questions 1–5 refer to Table 1.

TABLE 1: HALF-LIVES OF SEVERAL RADIOACTIVE NUCLIDES

Nuclide	Half-life
Manganese-56	3 h
Palladium-148	5 days
Silver-102	70 min
Zinc-62	9 h

_____ **1.** Which nuclide has a half-life of slightly more than 1 hr?
   a. manganese-56
   b. palladium-148
   c. silver-102
   d. zinc-62

_____ **2.** Which of the following nuclides is likely the most stable?
   a. manganese-56
   b. palladium-148
   c. silver-102
   d. zinc-62

_____ **3.** For equal masses of nuclides at the start, which nuclide would have the least mass after 5 hr?
   a. manganese-56
   b. palladium-148
   c. silver-102
   d. zinc-62

_____ **4.** What fraction of the original mass of palladium-138 will remain after 10 days?
   a. ½
   b. ⅓
   c. ¼
   d. ⅕

| Quiz *continued*

_____ **5.** For equal masses of nuclides at the start, how does the mass of zinc-62 compare with the mass of manganese-56 after 9 hr?
　　a. 1:3
　　b. 1:2
　　c. 4:1
　　d. 8:1

_____ **6.** A nuclide with which of the following half-lives would be appropriate to use to estimate the age of a rock from a rock formation believed to be 3 billion years old?
　　a. 2×10^3 years
　　b. 5×10^5 years
　　c. 8×10^6 years
　　d. 2×10^9 years

_____ **7.** Positron emission tomography (PET) is an application of what process?
　　a. electron capture
　　b. fission
　　c. fusion
　　d. positron emission

_____ **8.** Which statement is true concerning radiation exposure for humans?
　　a. All radiation exposures are lethal.
　　b. Acute exposure is more harmful than chronic exposure.
　　c. The curie (Cu) is the unit in which exposure to a dose of radiation is measured.
　　d. None of the above

_____ **9.** A rad is a measure of
　　a. radioactive decay.
　　b. exposure to ionizing radiation.
　　c. energy absorption caused by ionizing radiation.
　　d. biological effect of the absorbed dose in humans.

_____ **10.** Which of the following statements is true about film badges that are used to monitor radiation exposure.
　　a. Radiation causes chemical changes that are visible in the film.
　　b. The film is affected only by alpha particles.
　　c. The degree of darkening of the film indicates the total exposure to radiation.
　　d. Both (a) and (c)

Chapter Test

Nuclear Chemistry

In the space provided, write the letter of the term or phrase that best completes each statement or best answers each question.

_____ **1.** Which of the following reactions is a fission reaction?
  a. Hydrogen-2 and hydrogen-3 combine to form a helium-4 atom and a neutron.
  b. Carbon-12 and hydrogen-1 combine to form a nitrogen-13 atom.
  c. Uranium-235 absorbs a neutron and splits into barium-141, krypton-92, and three neutrons.
  d. A glucose molecule is metabolized with oxygen into carbon dioxide and water.

_____ **2.** The band of stability (shown in shaded area) is placed correctly on graph _____ in **Figure 1.**

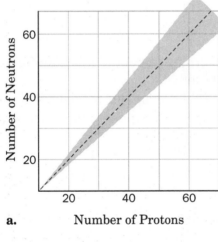

a.   Number of Protons

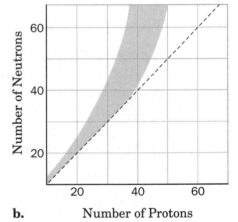

b.   Number of Protons

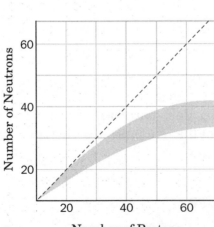

Figure 1 **c.**   Number of Protons

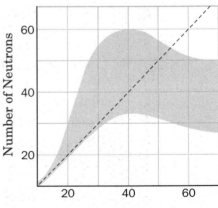

d.   Number of Protons

_____ **3.** The one-step transformation of $^{23}_{9}F$ from $^{23}_{10}Ne$ with the emission of gamma rays is an example of a(n)
   a. beta decay.
   b. electron capture.
   c. fission reaction.
   d. fusion reaction.

_____ **4.** Which of the following reactions is a fusion reaction?
   a. Uranium-236 absorbs a neutron and splits into lanthanum-139 and molybdenum-95 and 2 protons.
   b. Hydrogen and deuterium form helium-3.
   c. Carbon-14 decays into nitrogen-14 and a beta particle.
   d. Hydrogen and oxygen combine to form water.

_____ **5.** Three forms of nuclear radiation, ranked from most massive to least massive are
   a. alpha, beta, gamma.
   b. beta, gamma, alpha.
   c. gamma, alpha, beta.
   d. gamma, beta, alpha.

_____ **6.** Which of the following statements about neutron activation analysis is NOT true?
   a. It is used to diagnose medical disorders.
   b. It is used detect forged artwork.
   c. The neutrons transform elements in the sample into identifiable radioactive isotopes.
   d. It does not destroy the tested material.

_____ **7.** The most stable nuclei have an ____ number of protons and an ____ number of neutrons.
   a. even; odd
   b. even; even
   c. odd; even
   d. odd; odd

_____ **8.** After two half-lives, the amount of carbon-14 left in a 20-g sample would be ____ of the original amount.
   a. 50%
   b. 25%
   c. 20%
   d. 0%

_____ 9. All of the following are probable effects of radiation exposure *except*
  a. a decrease in white blood cells.
  b. loss of hair.
  c. death.
  d. muscle failure.

Isotope	Half-life	Isotope	Half-life
carbon-14	5.73×10^3 y	thorium-230	8.0×10^4 y
potassium-40	1.28×10^9 y	uranium-235	7.1×10^8 y
radium-226	1.6×10^3 y		

Figure 2

_____ 10. According to **Figure 2,** the radioactive isotope that would be appropriate to judge the age of a rock that is 1 billion years old is
  a. carbon-14.
  b. potassium-40.
  c. radium-226.
  d. thorium-230.

_____ 11. According to **Figure 2,** if a rock contains only 25% of the expected amount of uranium-235, it is _____ years old.
  a. 2.8×10^9
  b. 7.1×10^8
  c. 3.6×10^8
  d. 1.4×10^9

_____ 12. Based on half-life alone, which of the isotopes in **Figure 2** is the least stable?
  a. carbon-14
  b. potassiun-40
  c. radium-226
  d. thorium-230

_____ 13. The radiation with the greatest penetrating power consists of
  a. alpha particles.
  b. beta particles.
  c. gamma rays.
  d. positrons.

_____ 14. Which of the following equations describes an alpha emission?
  a. $^8_4Be + ^4_2He \rightarrow ^{12}_6C + \gamma$
  b. $^{235}_{92}U \rightarrow ^4_2He + ^{231}_{90}Th$
  c. $^{14}_7N + ^4_2He \rightarrow ^8_4Be \rightarrow ^{17}_8O + ^1_1H$
  d. $^3_1H + ^2_1H \rightarrow ^4_2He + ^1_0n + 2.8 \times 10^{-12}$ J

| Chapter Test *continued*

_____ **15.** A nuclear change results from all of the following *except*

    a. fusion.

    b. fission.

    c. a radioactive decay.

    d. a chemical reaction.

_____ **16.** Which of the following radioactive decay processes does NOT reduce the atomic number of a nuclide?

    a. alpha decay

    b. beta decay

    c. positron capture

    d. electron capture

_____ **17.** Which of the following general statements would account for instability of the nuclide $^{43}_{21}\text{Sc}$?

    a. Except for $^{1}_{1}\text{H}$ and $^{3}_{2}\text{He}$, a stable nucleus has N equal to or greater than Z.

    b. A stable nucleus has an $\dfrac{N}{Z}$ value between 1 and 1.5.

    c. A stable nucleus has 2, 8, 20, 28, 50, or 82 protons or neutrons.

    d. All nuclides that have Z greater than 83 and $(N + Z)$ greater than 209 are unstable.

_____ **18.** The strong force

    a. acts over a distance much smaller than the electrostatic repulsion.

    b. accounts for attraction between nucleons.

    c. can be stronger than the electrostatic repulsion.

    d. All of the above

_____ **19.** A decay series ends with a

    a. fissionable nuclide.

    b. positron emission.

    c. stable nuclide.

    d. transuranium element.

_____ **20.** A moderator in a nuclear reactor

    a. absorbs uranium-235 nuclei.

    b. converts thermal energy to electrical energy.

    c. provides energy for the reactor.

    d. slows down neutrons.

| **Chapter Test** *continued*

Answer the questions in the spaces provided.

21. Use the concepts of electrostatic repulsion and strong nuclear force to explain why some atoms decay.

_____

_____

22. Predict the product of the nuclear reaction shown in **Figure 3.** Refer to a periodic table.

Figure 3

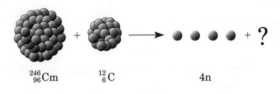

$$^{246}_{96}\text{Cm} \qquad ^{12}_{6}\text{C} \qquad\qquad 4\text{n}$$

_____

_____

_____

_____

_____

_____

Answer the following question on a separate piece of paper.

23. Explain in terms of nuclear force and electrostatic charge why nuclear stability increases for nuclei with atomic numbers lower than iron-56 and nickel-58 but decreases for atomic nuclei greater than iron-56 and nickel-58.

Answer each of the following problems in the spaces provided.

24. Complete and balance the following nuclear reactions by finding the missing product. Then describe the reaction. Refer to a periodic table if necessary.

$$^{4}_{2}\text{He} + ^{4}_{2}\text{He} \rightarrow ? + \gamma$$

_____

25. Write the nuclear equation for the beta decay of calcium-45. Refer to a periodic table if necessary.

Skills Practice Lab

OBSERVATION

Radioactivity

The types of radiation emitted by radioactive materials include alpha particles, beta particles, and gamma rays. Alpha particles are helium nuclei; beta particles are high-speed electrons; and gamma rays are extremely high-frequency photons. Alpha particles will discharge an electroscope, but their penetrating power is not great enough to affect a Geiger counter tube. A few centimeters of air will stop an alpha particle. Beta particles can be detected by a Geiger counter tube and can penetrate several centimeters of air, but several layers of paper or aluminum foil can stop them. Gamma rays can penetrate through several centimeters of concrete.

The environment contains a small amount of natural radiation, which can be detected by a Geiger counter. This is called background radiation and is primarily due to cosmic rays from stars. A small amount of background radiation may also come from the walls of buildings made of stone, clay, and some kinds of bricks, and from other sources such as dust particles.

OBJECTIVES

Use a Geiger counter to determine the level of background radiation.

Compare counts per minute for a beta source passing through air, index cards, and aluminum.

Graph data and determine the relationship between counts per minute and thickness of material.

Graph data and determine the effect of distance on counts per minute in air.

MATERIALS

- aluminum foil
- index cards
- radioactivity demonstrator (scaler)
- thallium 204 (beta source)

Always wear safety goggles and a lab apron to protect your eyes and clothing. If you get a chemical in your eyes, immediately flush the chemical out at the eyewash station while calling to your teacher. Know the location of the emergency lab shower and eyewash station and the procedures for using them.

Do not touch any chemicals. If you get a chemical on your skin or clothing, wash the chemical off at the sink while calling to your teacher. Make sure you carefully read the labels and follow the precautions on all containers of chemicals that you use. If there are no precautions stated on the label, ask your teacher what precautions to follow. Do not taste any chemicals or items used in the laboratory. Never return leftovers to their original container; take only small amounts to avoid wasting supplies.

Procedure
PART–BACKGROUND COUNT

CAUTION The wiring between the Geiger counter probe and the counter carries more than 1000 volts. Do not touch it when the equipment is operating or for at least 5 min after it has been unplugged from the electric socket.

1. Put on safety goggles, gloves, and lab apron.

2. Carefully read the directions on the operation of your counter. Set the counter to zero. Do not have any radioactive sources within 1 m of the Geiger counter tube. Turn on the counter for 1 min and count the frequency of clicks. Record the number of clicks per minute in **Table 1**. Repeat two more trials. The average of these trials will be your background count in counts per minute (cpm).

PART–RANGE OF BETA PARTICLES IN VARIOUS MEDIA

3. Air: Place the beta source approximately 5 cm from the Geiger tube. The proper setup is shown in **Figure 1**.
CAUTION You should never directly handle a radioactive source. Be certain you are wearing gloves when handling the beta source (thallium 204).

    Determine the count for 1 min, and record your count/per minute and distance between the source and Geiger tube in **Table 2**.

4. Move the source another 5 cm, and determine and record the count for 1 min. Continue this procedure until you reach the background count or have completed 10 trials.

Figure 1

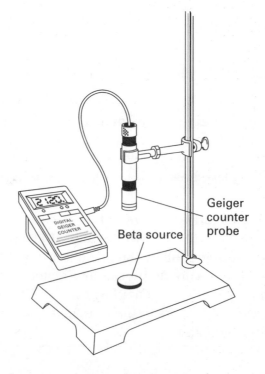

Geiger counter probe

Beta source

5. Paper: Place the beta source approximately 5 cm from the Geiger tube. Place a single index card on top of the beta source and determine the count for 1 min. Record the number of counts per minute in **Table 3.**

6. Keep the distance from the source to the Geiger tube constant, and repeat step **4** with an additional index card. Continue adding index cards and measuring and recording counts until the background count is reached or 10 trials have been completed.

7. Aluminum: Repeat steps **4** and **5,** but use sheets of aluminum foil in place of index cards. Record your data in **Table 3.**

8. Return the beta source to your teacher.

TABLE 1 BACKGROUND COUNT DATA

Background Count	
Trial	**Count/min**
1	data will vary
2	data will vary
3	data will vary
Average	data will vary

TABLE 2 RANGE OF BETA PARTICLES IN AIR

Air					
Distance (cm)	**Count/ min**	**Distance (cm)**	**Count/ min**	**Distance (cm)**	**Count/ min**

TABLE 3 PENETRATING POWER OF BETA PARTICLES

Index Cards		Aluminum	
No. Sheets	Count/min	No. Sheets	Count/min
0		0	
1		1	
2		2	
3		3	
4		4	
5		5	
6		6	
7		7	
8		8	
9		9	
10		10	

Analysis

1. **Organizing Data** On a separate piece of graph paper, plot a graph of counts per minute versus distance between the beta source and the Geiger tube. Subtract the background count from each of the readings. Place counts per minute on the vertical axis and the distance on the horizontal axis. Describe the relationship between distance and counts per minute.

_____

2. **Organizing Data** On a separate piece of graph paper, plot a graph of the number of index cards versus counts per minute. Place the counts per minute on the vertical axis. Describe the relationship between the number of index cards and counts per minute.

_____

_____

3. **Organizing Data** On a separate piece of graph paper, plot a graph of the number of sheets of aluminum foil versus counts per minute. Place the counts per minute on the vertical axis. Describe the relationship between the number of sheets of aluminum and counts per minute.

_____

_____

_____

Conclusions

1. **Analyzing Results** According to the three graphs, which substance is the most efficient absorber of beta particles? Explain how you made your decision.

_____

_____

2. **Relating Ideas** What is the implication of discovering a larger-than-normal amount of helium in a natural-gas well?

_____

_____

_____

_____

Name _____ Class _____ Date _____

OBSERVATION

Detecting Radioactivity

The element radon is the product of the radioactive decay of uranium. The $^{222}_{86}Rn$ nucleus is unstable and has a half-life of about 4 days. Radon decays by giving off alpha particles (helium nuclei) and beta particles (electrons) according to the equations below, with $^{4}_{2}He$ indicating an alpha particle and $^{0}_{-1}\beta$ representing a beta particle. Chemically, radon is a noble gas. Other noble gases can be inhaled without causing damage to the lungs because these gases are not radioactive. When radon is inhaled, however, it can rapidly decay into polonium, lead, and bismuth, all of which are solids that can lodge in body tissues and continue to decay. The lead isotope shown at the end of the chain of reactions, $^{210}_{82}Pb$, has a half-life of 22.6 years, and it will eventually undergo even more decay before creating the final stable product, $^{206}_{82}Pb$.

$$
\begin{aligned}
&^{222}_{86}Rn \\
&\quad\searrow \\
&\quad\quad ^{218}_{84}Po + {}^{4}_{2}He \\
&\quad\quad\quad\searrow \\
&\quad\quad\quad\quad ^{214}_{82}Pb + {}^{4}_{2}He \\
&\quad\quad\quad\quad\quad\searrow \\
&\quad\quad\quad\quad\quad\quad ^{214}_{83}Bi + {}^{0}_{-1}e \\
&\quad\quad\quad\quad\quad\quad\quad\searrow \\
&\quad\quad\quad\quad\quad\quad\quad\quad ^{214}_{84}Po + {}^{0}_{-1}e \\
&\quad\quad\quad\quad\quad\quad\quad\quad\quad\searrow \\
&\quad\quad\quad\quad\quad\quad\quad\quad\quad\quad ^{210}_{82}Pb + {}^{4}_{2}He \rightarrow
\end{aligned}
$$

In this experiment, you will measure the level of radon emissions in your community. First you will construct a simple detector using plastic (CR-39) that is sensitive to alpha particles. You will place the detector in your home or somewhere in your community for a 3 week period. Then, in the lab, the plastic will be etched with sodium hydroxide to make the tracks of the alpha particles visible. You will examine the tracks to determine the number of tracks per cm^2 per day and the activity of radon at the location. Finally, all class data will be pooled to make a map showing radon activity throughout your community.

OBJECTIVES

Build a radon detector and use it to detect radon emissions.

Observe the tracks of alpha particles microscopically and count them.

Calculate the activity of radon.

Evaluate radon activity over a large area using class data and draw a map of its activity.

| Detecting Radioactivity *continued*

MATERIALS

- clear plastic ruler or stage micrometer
- CR-39 plastic
- etch clamp (the ring from a key chain)
- index card, 3 in. × 5 in.
- microscope
- paper clips
- push pin
- scissors

- small plastic cup with lid
- tape
- toilet paper or other tissue

Optional
- sources of radiation (Fiestaware, Coleman green-label lantern mantles, old glow-in-the-dark clock or watch faces, cloud-chamber needles)

Always wear safety goggles and a lab apron to protect your eyes and clothing. If you get a chemical in your eyes, immediately flush the chemical out at the eyewash station while calling to your teacher. Know the location of the emergency lab shower and eyewash station and the procedures for using them.

 Scissors and push pins are sharp; use with care.

Procedure
PART 1–DETECTOR CONSTRUCTION

1. Put on safety goggles, gloves, and lab apron.

2. Cut a rectangle, 2 cm × 4 cm, from the index card.

3. Locate the side of the CR-39 plastic that has the felt-tip marker lines on it. Peel off the polyethylene film, and use the push pin to inscribe a number or other identification near the edge of the piece. With a short piece of transparent tape, form a loop with the sticky side out. Place the tape on the back of the piece of CR-39 plastic (the side that is still covered with polyethylene), and firmly attach it to the index-card rectangle.

4. With a permanent marker, write the ID number or other identification on the outside of the plastic cup. Place the paper rectangle, with the CR-39 plastic on top, into the cup.

5. Cut a hole in the center of the plastic-cup lid. Place a small piece of tissue over the top of the cup to serve as a dust filter. Then snap the lid onto the cup.

6. Place the completed detector in the location of your choice. (Check with your teacher first.) Record this information in **Table 1.** The detector must remain undisturbed at that location for at least 3 weeks.

7. At the end of the 3 weeks, return the entire detector to your teacher for the chemical-etching process and the counting of the radiation tracks.

| Detecting Radioactivity *continued*

PART 2–ETCHING

8. Remove the CR-39 plastic from the plastic cup, detach it from the index card, and peel the polyethylene film from the back. Slip the ring of an etch clamp over the top of the CR-39 plastic, and hook it onto a large paper clip that has been reshaped to have "hooks" at each end, as shown in **Figure 1.**

9. When you have completed this work, give the plastic to your teacher for the etching step. During this step, NaOH solution will be used to remove the outer layer of the plastic so that the tracks of the alpha particles become visible.

PART 3–COUNTING THE TRACKS

10. Examine **Figure 2** below. Notice the various shapes of the tracks left as alpha particles entered the CR-39 plastic. The circular tracks were formed by alpha particles that entered straight on, and the teardrop-shaped tracks were formed by alpha particles that entered at an angle.

Figure 1

11. Place your plastic sample under a microscope to view the tracks. Use a clear-plastic metric ruler or a stage micrometer to measure the diameter of the microscope's field of view. Make this measurement for low power (10×). Record this diameter in **Table 1.**

12. The tracks are on the top surface of the CR-39 plastic. Make certain that you focus on that surface and the tracks look like those in the illustration. These tracks were produced by placing the CR-39 plastic within a radium-coated clay urn. Your radon detector should not have nearly as many tracks. If there are too many tracks, switch to a high-power (40×) objective, and measure and record the diameter of the field of view. Place your piece of CR-39 plastic on a microscope slide. Count and record the number of tracks in 10 different fields. Record these numbers in **Table 2.**

Figure 2   Alpha particle tracks

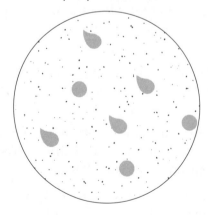

Detecting Radioactivity *continued*

TABLE 1 DETECTOR TIME AND LOCATION DATA

Date detector was put in place	
Time detector was put in place	
Location of detector (e.g., bedroom, kitchen, dining room, furnace room, under the stairwell, etc.)	
Floor level of location	
Date detector was removed	
Time detector was removed	
Diameter of microscope field	

TABLE 2 ALPHA PARTICLE TRACK DATA

Field										
Number of tracks										

Analysis

1. Organizing Data In order to increase the accuracy of your data, you counted tracks in 10 different areas. Find the average number of tracks in a single area for your piece of CR-39 plastic.

2. Organizing Data You counted the number of tracks within the field of view of your microscope. In order to calculate the number of tracks per cm^2, you need to know the area of the field. Use the diameter of the field to calculate the area. (Hint: The field is circular; $d = 2r$; $A = \pi r^2$.)

3. Organizing Data Using the answers to Analysis items **1** and **2,** calculate the average number of tracks per cm^2.

4. Organizing Data In Analysis item **3** you calculated the number of tracks that accumulated per cm^2 over the total period the detector was in place. Divide this number by the number of days the detector was in place to calculate tracks/cm^2/day.

5. Organizing Data Several pieces of CR-39 plastic were sent to a facility that had a radon chamber in which the activity of the radon was known to be 13.69 Bq/L (becquerels per liter of air), as measured by a different technique. A becquerel is the name for the SI unit of activity for a radioactive substance and is equal to 1 decay/s. The exposed pieces of CR-39 plastic were etched, counted, and found to have an activity of 2370 tracks/cm^2/day. Calculate the radon activity measured by your detector in becquerels/liter. (Hint: Use the proportion 13.69 Bq/L:2370 tracks/cm^2/day as a conversion factor to convert your data.)

6. Relating Ideas The Environmental Protection Agency and other U.S. government agencies use non-SI units of picocuries per liter (pCi/L) to measure radiation. One curie is 3.7×10^{10} Bq, and one picocurie is 10^{-12} curies. Convert your data into units of pCi/L.

7. Organizing Data Combine your data with those of other teams in your class, and jointly construct a map of your region that shows the levels of radon activity in Bq/L and pCi/L at various locations throughout your community.

Detecting Radioactivity *continued*

Conclusions

1. **Applying Ideas** The half-life of $^{222}_{86}\text{Rn}$ is 3.823 days. After what time will only one-fourth of a given amount of radon remain?

_____

_____

_____

_____

2. **Designing Experiments** Factors other than geographic location can have an effect on radon emissions. For example, readings taken in basements are likely to be higher than those in attics. Design an experiment to test different aspects of the three highest and three lowest regions of radiation on the map to examine the influence of these other factors. If your teacher approves your suggestion, try it.

_____

_____

_____

_____

3. **Designing Experiments** CR-39 plastic could be used for further investigations of naturally occurring radiation. Design an experiment to explore one of the following areas. If your teacher approves your plan, carry out the experiment.

   • the range of alpha particles

   • the radon activity in soil

   • radioactivity of common items such as lantern mantles (Coleman green label), glow-in-the-dark clock or watch faces, and pieces of Fiestaware

_____

_____

_____

_____

_____

Lesson Plan

Section: Atomic Nuclei and Nuclear Stability

Pacing

Regular Schedule   with lab(s): N/A   without lab(s): 1 day
Block Schedule   with lab(s): N/A   without lab(s): ½ day

Objectives

1. Describe how the strong force attracts nucleons.

2. Relate binding energy and mass defect.

3. Predict the stability of a nucleus by considering factors such as nuclear size, binding energy, and the ratio of neutrons to protons in the nucleus.

National Science Education Standards Covered

UNIFYING CONCEPTS AND PROCESSES

UCP 1 Systems, order, and organization

UCP 3 Change, constancy, and measurement

UCP 5 Form and function

PHYSICAL SCIENCE—STRUCTURE OF ATOMS

PS 1c The nuclear forces that hold the nucleus of an atom together, at nuclear distances, are usually stronger than the electric forces that would make it fly apart. Nuclear reactions convert a fraction of the mass of interacting particles into energy, and they can release much greater amounts of energy than atomic interactions. Fission is the splitting of a large nucleus into smaller pieces. Fusion is the joining of two nuclei at extremely high temperature and pressure, and is the process responsible for the energy of the sun and other stars.

PS 1d Radioactive isotopes are unstable and undergo spontaneous nuclear reactions, emitting particles and/or wavelike radiation. The decay of any one nucleus cannot be predicted, but a large group of identical nuclei decay at a predictable rate. This predictability can be used to estimate the age of materials that contain radioactive isotopes.

PHYSICAL SCIENCE—CONSERVATION OF ENERGY AND THE INCREASE IN DISORDER

PS 5a The total energy of the universe is constant. Energy can be transferred by collisions in chemical and nuclear reactions, by light waves and other radiations, and in many other ways. However, it can never be destroyed. As these transfers occur, the matter involved becomes steadily less ordered.

> **KEY**
> **SE** = Student Edition
> **ATE** = Annotated Teacher Edition

Block 1 *(45 minutes)*

FOCUS *5 minutes*

❑ **Bellringer,** ATE (GENERAL). This activity has students draw and label a picture of a helium atom.

MOTIVATE *10 minutes*

❑ **Activity** (GENERAL) Write the term *isotope* on the board. Ask students to define this term and give an example. (Students should recall that isotopes are atoms that have the same atomic number but different numbers of neutrons. Examples include carbon-12 and carbon-14.) Then, review the parts of the periodic table using a wall-sized periodic table or an overhead transparency. Have students relate the arrangement of the elements on the table to the number of protons and electrons in each type of atom. Point out that in this chapter, they will need to use isotopic atomic masses—not average atomic masses—later in this section (when calculating mass defect).

❑ **Demonstration,** ATE (GENERAL). This demonstration illustrates the difference between electrostatic attraction and electrostatic repulsion.

TEACH *20 minutes*

❑ **Reading Skill Builder,** ATE (BASIC). This feature has pairs of students read the section on atomic nuclei and nuclear stability. Then, the students alternate asking each other questions from the list provided.

❑ **Using the Figure,** ATE (GENERAL). Have students use Figure 4, which illustrates mass defect, to determine which of two isotopes has the greater mass defect, Te-122 or Te-128.

❑ **Using the Figure,** ATE (GENERAL). This feature uses the graph in Figure 5 (which shows the relative stability of nuclei) to discuss binding energies. Point out that the figure shows binding energy per nucleon, not total binding energy.

CLOSE *10 minutes*

❑ **Reteaching,** ATE (BASIC). Have students compare the strengths of the four fundamental forces in a table.

❑ **Quiz,** ATE (GENERAL). This assignment has students answer questions about the concepts in this lesson.

❑ **Assessment Worksheet: Section Quiz** (GENERAL)

HOMEWORK

❑ **Section Review,** SE (GENERAL). Assign items 1–12.

❑ **Skills Worksheet: Concept Review** (GENERAL)

OTHER RESOURCES

❑ **Group Activity,** ATE (ADVANCED). This activity has students research quarks and quark theory.

❑ **Homework,** ATE (ADVANCED). This assignment provides additional practice calculating binding energy.

❑ **Focus on Graphing,** SE (GENERAL)

❑ **go.hrw.com**

❑ **www.scilinks.org**

Lesson Plan

Section: Nuclear Change

Pacing

Regular Schedule	**with lab(s):** 3 days	**without lab(s):** 2 days
Block Schedule	**with lab(s):** 1½ days	**without lab(s):** 1 day

Objectives

1. Predict the particles and electromagnetic waves produced by different types of radioactive decay, and write equations for nuclear decays.

2. Identify examples of nuclear fission, and describe potential benefits and hazards of its use.

3. Describe nuclear fusion and its potential as an energy source.

National Science Education Standards Covered

UNIFYING CONCEPTS AND PROCESSES

UCP 1 Systems, order, and organization

UCP 3 Change, constancy, and measurement

UCP 5 Form and function

PHYSICAL SCIENCE—STRUCTURE OF ATOMS

PS 1c The nuclear forces that hold the nucleus of an atom together, at nuclear distances, are usually stronger than the electric forces that would make it fly apart. Nuclear reactions convert a fraction of the mass of interacting particles into energy, and they can release much greater amounts of energy than atomic interactions. Fission is the splitting of a large nucleus into smaller pieces. Fusion is the joining of two nuclei at extremely high temperature and pressure, and is the process responsible for the energy of the sun and other stars.

PS 1d Radioactive isotopes are unstable and undergo spontaneous nuclear reactions, emitting particles and/or wavelike radiation. The decay of any one nucleus cannot be predicted, but a large group of identical nuclei decay at a predictable rate. This predictability can be used to estimate the age of materials that contain radioactive isotopes.

PHYSICAL SCIENCE—CONSERVATION OF ENERGY AND THE INCREASE IN DISORDER

PS 5a The total energy of the universe is constant. Energy can be transferred by collisions in chemical and nuclear reactions, by light waves and other radiations, and in many other ways. However, it can never be destroyed. As these transfers occur, the matter involved becomes steadily less ordered.

> **KEY**
> **SE** = Student Edition
> **ATE** = Annotated Teacher Edition

Block 2 *(45 minutes)*

FOCUS *5 minutes*

❑ **Bellringer,** ATE (GENERAL). This activity has students write a short paragraph about nuclear power plants.

MOTIVATE *10 minutes*

❑ **Activity** (GENERAL) Show students a graph of neutron-proton ratios of stable nuclei. (For example, you could use the graph found in Figure 6 on page 644 of the textbook.) Remind students that the graph shows the band of stability (the area on the graph where stable nuclei are found). Then ask students to propose different ways an unstable nucleus could get in the band of stability. (An atom can gain or lose protons, gain or lose neutrons, or gain or lose both neutrons and protons.) Link students' answers to Table 1 in the student textbook.

TEACH *30 minutes*

❑ **Demonstration,** ATE (GENERAL). This demonstration shows how a Geiger-Mueller counter detects beta radiation.

❑ **Using the Figure,** ATE (GENERAL). Students determine the different kinds of decay shown for each isotope represented by color-coded arrows in Figure 10.

❑ **Skills Toolkit: Balancing Nuclear Equations,** SE (GENERAL). Take students through the steps of balancing a nuclear equation.

❑ **Sample Problem A: Balancing a Nuclear Equation,** SE (GENERAL). This problem demonstrates how to balance nuclear equations.

❑ **Observation Lab: Radioactivity,** Chapter Resource File (GENERAL). Students use a Geiger counter to compare the counts per minute for a beta source passing through air, index cards, and aluminum. Then, they graph and analyze their data.

HOMEWORK

❑ **Practice Sample Problems A,** SE (GENERAL). Balancing a Nuclear Equation. Assign items 1–4.

❑ **Homework,** ATE (BASIC). This assignment has students construct a table to organize the information about radioactive decays.

❑ **Homework,** ATE (GENERAL). This assignment gives students additional practice balancing nuclear equations.

| Lesson Plan *continued*

OTHER RESOURCES

❏ **Group Activity,** ATE (BASIC). Students construct a model that can be used to show radioactive decay.

❏ **Skill Builder,** ATE (ADVANCED). Have students research food irradiation.

❏ **go.hrw.com**

❏ **www.scilinks.org**

Block 3 *(45 minutes)*

TEACH *30 minutes*

❏ **Demonstration,** ATE (GENERAL). This demonstration shows a chain reaction using dominoes.

❏ **Using the Figure,** ATE (GENERAL). Trace the events shown in Figure 11 and help students visualize the ratio of neutron release during a collision event is 1:3:9:27:81:243, and so on.

❏ **Transparency,** Model of a Pressurized, Light-Water Nuclear Reactor (GEN-ERAL). This transparency shows the parts of a nuclear reactor like those commonly used to generate electricity in the United States. (Figure 12)

❏ **Using the Figure,** ATE (GENERAL). This activity has students locate the three water systems in the nuclear reactor shown in Figure 12.

❏ **Misconception Alert,** ATE (GENERAL). Ask whether an accident in the nuclear reactor in Figure 12 could result in a nuclear explosion like that of a nuclear bomb. Discuss the meaning and consequences of a nuclear meltdown.

CLOSE *15 minutes*

❏ **Reteaching,** ATE (BASIC). Students create a concept map of the concepts in this section.

❏ **Quiz,** ATE (GENERAL). This assignment has students answer questions about the concepts in this lesson.

❏ **Assessment Worksheet: Section Quiz** (GENERAL)

HOMEWORK

❏ **Section Review,** SE (GENERAL). Assign items 1–10.

❏ **Skills Worksheet: Concept Review** (GENERAL)

OTHER RESOURCES

❏ **Teaching Tip,** ATE (ADVANCED). Have students research the history of "cold fusion" and summarize their findings in a poster.

❏ **go.hrw.com**

❏ **www.scilinks.org**

Lesson Plan

Section: Uses of Nuclear Chemistry

Pacing

Regular Schedule   **with lab(s):** 4 days   **without lab(s):** 2 days

Block Schedule   **with lab(s):** 2 days   **without lab(s):** 1 day

Objectives

1. Define the half-life of a radioactive nuclide, and explain how it can be used to determine an object's age.

2. Describe some of the uses of nuclear chemistry.

3. Compare acute and chronic exposure to radiation.

National Science Education Standards Covered

UNIFYING CONCEPTS AND PROCESSES

UCP 1 Systems, order, and organization

UCP 3 Change, constancy, and measurement

UCP 5 Form and function

PHYSICAL SCIENCE—STRUCTURE OF ATOMS

PS 1d Radioactive isotopes are unstable and undergo spontaneous nuclear reactions, emitting particles and/or wavelike radiation. The decay of any one nucleus cannot be predicted, but a large group of identical nuclei decay at a predictable rate. This predictability can be used to estimate the age of materials that contain radioactive isotopes.

PHYSICAL SCIENCE—CONSERVATION OF ENERGY AND THE INCREASE IN DISORDER

PS 5a The total energy of the universe is constant. Energy can be transferred by collisions in chemical and nuclear reactions, by light waves and other radiations, and in many other ways. However, it can never be destroyed. As these transfers occur, the matter involved becomes steadily less ordered.

KEY
SE = Student Edition
ATE = Annotated Teacher Edition

Block 4 (45 minutes)

FOCUS 10 minutes

❑ **Bellringer,** ATE (GENERAL). Students write a paragraph stating their opinion about the benefits or dangers of radioactivity. Allow students to share their opinions with the class.

| Lesson Plan *continued*

MOTIVATE *10 minutes*

❑ **Demonstration,** ATE (GENERAL). Show students an X ray image from an MRI or CT scan and discuss the uses of radiation in medical imaging. Invite students to share any experiences they or someone they know might have had with one of these forms of imaging.

TEACH *25 minutes*

❑ **Teaching Tip: Rate of Decay,** ATE (BASIC). Use this series of questions to compare the rates of chemical reactions with the rates of radioactive decay.

❑ **Sample Problem B: Determining the Age of an Artifact,** SE (GENERAL). This problem demonstrates how to determine the age of an artifact.

❑ **Using the Figure,** ATE (GENERAL). Use this item along with Figure 16 to discuss the uses of carbon-14 dating.

❑ **Transparency,** Rate of Decay of Potassium-40. This transparency illustrates the rate of decay of potassium-40. (GENERAL) (Figure 17)

HOMEWORK

❑ **Practice Sample Problems B,** SE (GENERAL). Determining the Age of an Artifact. Assign items 1–3.

❑ **Homework,** ATE (GENERAL). This assignment gives students additional practice determining the age of artifacts.

OTHER RESOURCES

❑ **go.hrw.com**

❑ **www.scilinks.org**

Block 5 *(45 minutes)*

TEACH *35 minutes*

❑ **Sample Problem C: Determining the Original Mass of a Sample,** SE (GENERAL). This problem demonstrates how to determine the original mass of a sample.

❑ **Demonstration,** ATE (GENERAL). This demonstration illustrates how an ionizing smoke detector works.

❑ **Teaching Tip,** ATE (GENERAL). Use Figure 19 and this item to compare a PET scan to the other imaging scans discussed in this section. Take students through the steps in this item to explain how a PET scan is produced.

❑ **Observation Lab: Detecting Radioactivity,** Chapter Resource File (GENERAL). Students build a radon detector and use it to detect radon emissions. They also observe the tracks of alpha particles, collect and pool their data with that of classmates, and then analyze the data.

| Lesson Plan *continued*

CLOSE *10 minutes*

❑ **Reteaching,** ATE (BASIC). Students write an article about a positive use of nuclear chemistry.

❑ **Quiz,** ATE (GENERAL). This assignment has students answer questions about the concepts in this lesson.

❑ **Assessment Worksheet: Section Quiz** (GENERAL)

HOMEWORK

❑ **Practice Sample Problems C,** SE (GENERAL). Determining the Original Mass of a Sample. Assign items 1–3.

❑ **Homework,** ATE (GENERAL). This assignment gives students additional practice determining the original mass of a sample.

❑ **Section Review,** SE (GENERAL). Assign items 1–11.

❑ **Skills Worksheet: Concept Review** (GENERAL)

OTHER RESOURCES

❑ **Teaching Tip,** ATE (ADVANCED). Students make a model or a poster of the reactions involved in neutron activation analysis.

❑ **Skill Builder,** ATE (GENERAL). Allow students to research different kinds of radiological medical treatments and share the results of their research with the class.

❑ **go.hrw.com**

❑ **www.scilinks.org**

END OF CHAPTER REVIEW AND ASSESSMENT RESOURCES

❑ **Mixed Review,** SE (GENERAL).

❑ **Alternate Assessment,** SE (GENERAL).

❑ **Technology and Learning,** SE (GENERAL).

❑ **Standardized Text Prep,** SE (GENERAL).

❑ **Assessment Worksheet: Chapter Test** (GENERAL)

❑ **Test Item Listing for ExamView® Test Generator**

OBSERVATION

Radioactivity

Teacher Notes

TIME REQUIRED One 45-minute lab period

SKILLS ACQUIRED
Collecting data
Communicating
Inferring
Interpreting
Organizing and analyzing data

RATING
Easy ← 1   2   3   4 → Hard

Teacher Prep–2
Student Set-Up–2
Concept Level–2
Clean Up–2

THE SCIENTIFIC METHOD

Make Observations Students collect data on the properties of beta particles.

Analyze the Results Analysis questions 1 to 3 and Conclusions question 1

Draw Conclusions Conclusions questions 1 and 2

Communicate the Results Analysis questions 1–3 and Conclusions question 1

MATERIALS

Thallium 204 is an inexpensive beta source with a useful life of about 15 years. Read the special precautions about radioactive sources.

A decade scaler is an ideal radioactive counter. Thorton has an excellent scaler that is one of the least-expensive models available.

SAFETY CAUTIONS

Before your students perform this experiment, you should read the manufacturer's precautions for the use of the counter equipment. Be sure you and your students understand and follow all the precautions. Similarly, be sure you and your students will follow the supplier's precautions for the use and handling of the beta source. When not in use, the beta source should be kept secure in a locked location not accessible to students.

Remind students of the following safety precautions:

• Always wear safety goggles and a lab apron to protect your eyes and clothing. If you get a chemical in your eyes, immediately flush the chemical out at the eyewash station while calling to your teacher. Know the location of the emergency lab shower and the eyewash stations and procedures for using them.

Radioactivity *continued*

- Do not touch any chemicals. If you get a chemical on your skin or clothing, wash the chemical off at the sink while calling to your teacher. Make sure you carefully read the labels and follow the precautions on all containers of chemicals that you use. If there are no precautions stated on the label, ask your teacher what precautions you should follow. Do not taste any chemicals or items used in the laboratory. Never return leftovers to their original containers; take only small amounts to avoid wasting supplies.

- Call your teacher in the event of a spill. Spills should be cleaned up promptly, according to your teacher's directions.

- Never put broken glass in a regular waste container. Broken glass should be disposed of properly.

DISPOSAL

Students must return the beta emitter to you for safe storage as described under Safety Cautions.

TECHNIQUES TO DEMONSTRATE

Be sure that students understand how to use the counter according to the directions accompanying your counters. Show students how to set up the counter and Beta source for measurement. Require that they measure the distances to $\pm$ 1 cm.

TIPS AND TRICKS

Ask students why it is necessary to determine a background count and subtract it from the values they obtain when measuring the output of the Beta emitter.

Discuss the graphing of data and what the slope of a straight line means when assessing the dependence of one variable on another.

Skills Practice Lab   **OBSERVATION**

Radioactivity

The types of radiation emitted by radioactive materials include alpha particles, beta particles, and gamma rays. Alpha particles are helium nuclei; beta particles are high-speed electrons; and gamma rays are extremely high-frequency photons. Alpha particles will discharge an electroscope, but their penetrating power is not great enough to affect a Geiger counter tube. A few centimeters of air will stop an alpha particle. Beta particles can be detected by a Geiger counter tube and can penetrate several centimeters of air, but several layers of paper or aluminum foil can stop them. Gamma rays can penetrate through several centimeters of concrete.

The environment contains a small amount of natural radiation, which can be detected by a Geiger counter. This is called background radiation and is primarily due to cosmic rays from stars. A small amount of background radiation may also come from the walls of buildings made of stone, clay, and some kinds of bricks, and from other sources such as dust particles.

OBJECTIVES

Use a Geiger counter to determine the level of background radiation.

Compare counts per minute for a beta source passing through air, index cards, and aluminum.

Graph data and determine the relationship between counts per minute and thickness of material.

Graph data and determine the effect of distance on counts per minute in air.

MATERIALS

• aluminum foil

• index cards

• radioactivity demonstrator (scaler)

• thallium 204 (beta source)

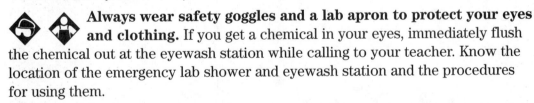

Always wear safety goggles and a lab apron to protect your eyes and clothing. If you get a chemical in your eyes, immediately flush the chemical out at the eyewash station while calling to your teacher. Know the location of the emergency lab shower and eyewash station and the procedures for using them.

Do not touch any chemicals. If you get a chemical on your skin or clothing, wash the chemical off at the sink while calling to your teacher. Make sure you carefully read the labels and follow the precautions on all containers of chemicals that you use. If there are no precautions stated on the label, ask your teacher what precautions to follow. Do not taste any chemicals or items used in the laboratory. Never return leftovers to their original container; take only small amounts to avoid wasting supplies.

| Radioactivity *continued*

Procedure

PART–BACKGROUND COUNT

CAUTION The wiring between the Geiger counter probe and the counter carries more than 1000 volts. Do not touch it when the equipment is operating or for at least 5 min after it has been unplugged from the electric socket.

1. Put on safety goggles, gloves, and lab apron.

2. Carefully read the directions on the operation of your counter. Set the counter to zero. Do not have any radioactive sources within 1 m of the Geiger counter tube. Turn on the counter for 1 min and count the frequency of clicks. Record the number of clicks per minute in **Table 1.** Repeat two more trials. The average of these trials will be your background count in counts per minute (cpm).

PART–RANGE OF BETA PARTICLES IN VARIOUS MEDIA

3. Air: Place the beta source approximately 5 cm from the Geiger tube. The proper setup is shown in **Figure 1.**
   CAUTION You should never directly handle a radioactive source. Be certain you are wearing gloves when handling the beta source (thallium 204).
   Determine the count for 1 min, and record your count/per minute and distance between the source and Geiger tube in **Table 2.**

4. Move the source another 5 cm, and determine and record the count for 1 min. Continue this procedure until you reach the background count or have completed 10 trials.

Figure 1

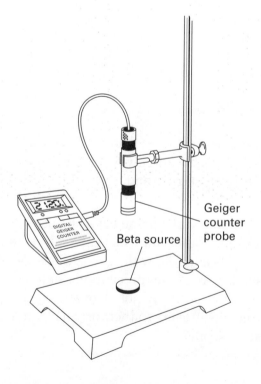

Beta source

Geiger
counter
probe

DIGITAL
GEIGER
COUNTER

Name _____   Class _____   Date _____

Radioactivity *continued*

5. Paper: Place the beta source approximately 5 cm from the Geiger tube. Place a single index card on top of the beta source and determine the count for 1 min. Record the number of counts per minute in **Table 3.**

6. Keep the distance from the source to the Geiger tube constant, and repeat step **4** with an additional index card. Continue adding index cards and measuring and recording counts until the background count is reached or 10 trials have been completed.

7. Aluminum: Repeat steps **4** and **5,** but use sheets of aluminum foil in place of index cards. Record your data in **Table 3.**

8. Return the beta source to your teacher.

TABLE 1 BACKGROUND COUNT DATA

Background Count	
Trial	**Count/min**
1	data will vary
2	data will vary
3	data will vary
Average	data will vary

TABLE 2 RANGE OF BETA PARTICLES IN AIR

Air					
Distance (cm)	**Count/ min**	**Distance (cm)**	**Count/ min**	**Distance (cm)**	**Count/ min**

Radioactivity *continued*

TABLE 3 PENETRATING POWER OF BETA PARTICLES

Index Cards		Aluminum	
No. Sheets	Count/min	No. Sheets	Count/min
0		0	
1		1	
2		2	
3		3	
4		4	
5		5	
6		6	
7		7	
8		8	
9		9	
10		10	

Analysis

1. **Organizing Data** On a separate piece of graph paper, plot a graph of counts per minute versus distance between the beta source and the Geiger tube. Subtract the background count from each of the readings. Place counts per minute on the vertical axis and the distance on the horizontal axis. Describe the relationship between distance and counts per minute.

   The graph shows an inverse relationship. _____

2. **Organizing Data** On a separate piece of graph paper, plot a graph of the number of index cards versus counts per minute. Place the counts per minute on the vertical axis. Describe the relationship between the number of index cards and counts per minute.

   The graph shows an inverse relationship. _____

   _____

3. **Organizing Data** On a separate piece of graph paper, plot a graph of the number of sheets of aluminum foil versus counts per minute. Place the counts per minute on the vertical axis. Describe the relationship between the number of sheets of aluminum and counts per minute.

   The graph shows an inverse relationship. _____

   _____

   _____

Name _____ Class _____ Date _____

Radioactivity *continued*

Conclusions

1. Analyzing Results According to the three graphs, which substance is the most efficient absorber of beta particles? Explain how you made your decision.

Aluminum; the slope of the line is the least when aluminum foil is used.

_____

2. Relating Ideas What is the implication of discovering a larger-than-normal amount of helium in a natural-gas well?

A higher concentration of helium in natural gas could mean that there is a

higher-than-normal concentration of radioactive material in that location.

_____

_____

OBSERVATION

Detecting Radioactivity

Teacher Notes

TIME REQUIRED Two 45-minute lab periods (with exposure time of 3 weeks—can be shortened with a source of alpha particles)

SKILLS ACQUIRED
Collecting data
Communicating
Designing experiments
Inferring
Interpreting
Measuring
Organizing and analyzing data

RATING

Easy  Hard

Teacher Prep–3
Student Set-Up–3
Concept Level–3
Clean Up–3

THE SCIENTIFIC METHOD

Make Observations Students build a radon detector and observe the tracks of alpha particles

Test the Hypothesis Conclusions questions 2 and 3

Analyze the Results Analysis questions 1 to 7

Draw Conclusions Conclusions question 1

Communicate the Results Analysis questions 1 to 7 and Conclusion question 1

MATERIALS

For teacher use only

• 10 mL, 6.25 M NaOH, per lab group

• 1000 mL beaker or 400 mL beakers, 2

• Bunsen burner or hot plate

• small test tube, 1 per lab group

To prepare 1 L of 6.25 M NaOH, observe the required safety precautions. Slowly and with stirring, dissolve 250.0 g of NaOH in 750 mL of distilled water. Then, after the solution has cooled, add enough distilled water to make 1 L of solution. The NaOH solution will get hot as the pellets dissolve. To prevent boiling and splattering, add the pellets a few at a time with stirring.

    An empty film canister can be used in place of the small plastic cup with lid.

    CR-39 plastic is available from Alpha Trak, 141 Northridge Drive, Centralia, WA 98531, (206) 736-3884.

Detecting Radioactivity *continued*

SAFETY CAUTIONS

Read all safety cautions, and discuss them with your students.

Students should not handle NaOH solutions with concentrations greater than 1.0 M.

Wear safety goggles, a face shield, impermeable gloves, and a lab apron when you prepare and use the 6.25 M NaOH for the etching step. Work in a hood known to be in operating condition and have another person present nearby to call for help in case of an emergency. Be sure you are within a 30 s walk of a safety shower and eyewash station known to be in good operating condition.

If students observe the etching process, they should wear safety goggles, a face shield, and a lab apron, and they should stand at least 5 ft from the caustic solution.

If students use radioactive sources, they must wear impermeable disposable gloves when handling these objects. "One-size-fits-all" polyethylene gloves are available at most grocery stores. The gloves should be removed by turning them inside out as they are taken off the hand and fingers. Keep them inside out when disposing of them in the trash can.

In case of a NaOH spill, first dilute with water. Then mop up the spill with wet cloths or a wet cloth mop while wearing disposable plastic gloves.

Remind students of the following safety precautions:

- Always wear safety goggles and a lab apron to protect your eyes and clothing. If you get a chemical in your eyes, immediately flush the chemical out at the eyewash station while calling to your teacher. Know the location of the emergency lab shower and the eyewash stations and procedures for using them.

- Do not touch any chemicals. If you get a chemical on your skin or clothing, wash the chemical off at the sink while calling to your teacher. Make sure you carefully read the labels and follow the precautions on all containers of chemicals that you use. If there are no precautions stated on the label, ask your teacher what precautions you should follow. Do not taste any chemicals or items used in the laboratory. Never return leftovers to their original containers; take only small amounts to avoid wasting supplies.

- Call your teacher in the event of a spill. Spills should be cleaned up promptly, according to your teacher's directions.

- Never put broken glass in a regular waste container. Broken glass should be disposed of properly.

- Scissors and push pins are sharp; use with care.

DISPOSAL

Neutralize waste NaOH solution by adding 1.0 M acid slowly, while stirring, until the pH is between 5 and 9. After checking that the pH is in this neutral range, the solution may be poured down the drain. Save the etched plastic for examination by students next year.

TECHNIQUES TO DEMONSTRATE

Either demonstrate how to build the detector, or have one on hand for students to examine.

You should not need to explain the usage of the microscope, but students will need help measuring and calculating the field of view. Also be certain that they focus the microscope on the proper level of the plastic.

TIPS AND TRICKS

If students observe the etching process, they should wear safety goggles, a face shield, and a lab apron, and they should stand at least 5 ft from the caustic solution.

Pour enough 6.25 M NaOH into each test tube so that the plastic will be completely immersed when the paper clip is hooked over the test tube's edge.

Check the paper clip and etch clamp to be certain the students have attached them properly to the CR-39 plastic.

Hook the paper clip over the test tube lip so that the CR-39 plastic is completely immersed in the NaOH.

Add water to the beaker(s). Place the test tubes in the water.

Heat the water bath to boiling, and boil for about 30 min. The water may have to be replenished periodically.

Carefully remove the CR-39 from the hot-water bath, and rinse it thoroughly. Dry the plastic with a soft tissue.

Thoroughly discuss all safety precautions outlined in this laboratory and in the safety section. Radioactivity is a poorly understood topic, so take this opportunity to discuss practical ways to reduce exposure.

Discuss how the properties of radon as a gas cause problems in airtight buildings.

Explain that the CR-39 plastic is covered with the polyethylene tape to protect it from radiation until it is ready for use. The NaOH bath strips away a thin layer of the plastic to expose the pathway of the alpha particles.

Discuss the calculations for Bq/L before the students make the calculations themselves. They often do not realize that *activity* = 2373 tracks/cm^2/day was determined as a standard from 370 pCi/L of air (13.69 Bq/L). The standard was used to calculate unknown concentrations of radon.

Skills Practice Lab

Detecting Radioactivity

The element radon is the product of the radioactive decay of uranium. The $^{222}_{86}Rn$ nucleus is unstable and has a half-life of about 4 days. Radon decays by giving off alpha particles (helium nuclei) and beta particles (electrons) according to the equations below, with $^{4}_{2}He$ indicating an alpha particle and $_{-1}^{0}\beta$ representing a beta particle. Chemically, radon is a noble gas. Other noble gases can be inhaled without causing damage to the lungs because these gases are not radioactive. When radon is inhaled, however, it can rapidly decay into polonium, lead, and bismuth, all of which are solids that can lodge in body tissues and continue to decay. The lead isotope shown at the end of the chain of reactions, $^{210}_{82}Pb$, has a half-life of 22.6 years, and it will eventually undergo even more decay before creating the final stable product, $^{206}_{82}Pb$.

$$^{222}_{86}Rn$$
$$\searrow$$
$$^{218}_{84}Po + {}^{4}_{2}He$$
$$\searrow$$
$$^{214}_{82}Pb + {}^{4}_{2}He$$
$$\searrow$$
$$^{214}_{83}Bi + {}^{0}_{-1}e$$
$$\searrow$$
$$^{214}_{84}Po + {}^{0}_{-1}e$$
$$\searrow$$
$$^{210}_{82}Pb + {}^{4}_{2}He \rightarrow$$

In this experiment, you will measure the level of radon emissions in your community. First you will construct a simple detector using plastic (CR-39) that is sensitive to alpha particles. You will place the detector in your home or somewhere in your community for a 3 week period. Then, in the lab, the plastic will be etched with sodium hydroxide to make the tracks of the alpha particles visible. You will examine the tracks to determine the number of tracks per cm^2 per day and the activity of radon at the location. Finally, all class data will be pooled to make a map showing radon activity throughout your community.

OBJECTIVES

Build a radon detector and use it to detect radon emissions.

Observe the tracks of alpha particles microscopically and count them.

Calculate the activity of radon.

Evaluate radon activity over a large area using class data and draw a map of its activity.

MATERIALS

- clear plastic ruler or stage micrometer
- CR-39 plastic
- etch clamp (the ring from a key chain)
- index card, 3 in. × 5 in.
- microscope
- paper clips
- push pin
- scissors

- small plastic cup with lid
- tape
- toilet paper or other tissue

Optional
- sources of radiation (Fiestaware, Coleman green-label lantern mantles, old glow-in-the-dark clock or watch faces, cloud-chamber needles)

 Always wear safety goggles and a lab apron to protect your eyes and clothing. If you get a chemical in your eyes, immediately flush the chemical out at the eyewash station while calling to your teacher. Know the location of the emergency lab shower and eyewash station and the procedures for using them.

Scissors and push pins are sharp; use with care.

Procedure

PART 1–DETECTOR CONSTRUCTION

1. Put on safety goggles, gloves, and lab apron.

2. Cut a rectangle, 2 cm × 4 cm, from the index card.

3. Locate the side of the CR-39 plastic that has the felt-tip marker lines on it. Peel off the polyethylene film, and use the push pin to inscribe a number or other identification near the edge of the piece. With a short piece of transparent tape, form a loop with the sticky side out. Place the tape on the back of the piece of CR-39 plastic (the side that is still covered with polyethylene), and firmly attach it to the index-card rectangle.

4. With a permanent marker, write the ID number or other identification on the outside of the plastic cup. Place the paper rectangle, with the CR-39 plastic on top, into the cup.

5. Cut a hole in the center of the plastic-cup lid. Place a small piece of tissue over the top of the cup to serve as a dust filter. Then snap the lid onto the cup.

6. Place the completed detector in the location of your choice. (Check with your teacher first.) Record this information in **Table 1.** The detector must remain undisturbed at that location for at least 3 weeks.

7. At the end of the 3 weeks, return the entire detector to your teacher for the chemical-etching process and the counting of the radiation tracks.

| Detecting Radioactivity *continued*

PART 2–ETCHING

8. Remove the CR-39 plastic from the plastic cup, detach it from
the index card, and peel the polyethylene film from the back.
Slip the ring of an etch clamp over the top of the CR-39 plastic,
and hook it onto a large paper clip that has been reshaped to
have "hooks" at each end, as shown in **Figure 1.**

9. When you have completed this work, give the plastic to your
teacher for the etching step. During this step, NaOH solution
will be used to remove the outer layer of the plastic so that the
tracks of the alpha particles become visible.

PART 3–COUNTING THE TRACKS

10. Examine **Figure 2** below. Notice the various shapes of the
tracks left as alpha particles entered the CR-39 plastic. The
circular tracks were formed by alpha particles that entered
straight on, and the teardrop-shaped tracks were formed by
alpha particles that entered at an angle.

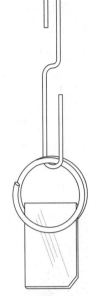

Figure 1

11. Place your plastic sample under a microscope to view the
tracks. Use a clear-plastic metric ruler or a stage micrometer to
measure the diameter of the microscope's field of view. Make this measurement for low power (10×). Record this diameter in **Table 1.**

12. The tracks are on the top surface of the CR-39 plastic. Make certain that you
focus on that surface and the tracks look like those in the illustration. These
tracks were produced by placing the CR-39 plastic within a radium-coated
clay urn. Your radon detector should not have nearly as many tracks. If there
are too many tracks, switch to a high-power (40×) objective, and measure
and record the diameter of the field of view. Place your piece of CR-39 plastic
on a microscope slide. Count and record the number of tracks in 10 different
fields. Record these numbers in **Table 2.**

Figure 2

Alpha particle tracks

❚ Detecting Radioactivity *continued*

TABLE 1 DETECTOR TIME AND LOCATION DATA

Date detector was put in place	**12/3/04**
Time detector was put in place	**3:45 PM**
Location of detector (e.g., bedroom, kitchen, dining room, furnace room, under the stairwell, etc.)	**kitchen**
Floor level of location	**1st**
Date detector was removed	**12/27/04**
Time detector was removed	**8:15 PM**
Diameter of microscope field	**Data will vary.**

TABLE 2 ALPHA PARTICLE TRACK DATA

Field	1	2	3	4	5	6	7	8	9	10
Number of tracks	3	4	4	5	9	7	4	3	8	6

Analysis

1. **Organizing Data** In order to increase the accuracy of your data, you counted tracks in 10 different areas. Find the average number of tracks in a single area for your piece of CR-39 plastic.

$$\frac{3 + 4 + 4 + 5 + 9 + 7 + 4 + 3 + 8 + 6}{10 \text{ fields}} = 5.3 \text{ tracks/field on average}$$

2. **Organizing Data** You counted the number of tracks within the field of view of your microscope. In order to calculate the number of tracks per cm^2, you need to know the area of the field. Use the diameter of the field to calculate the area. (Hint: The field is circular; $d = 2r$; $A = \pi r^2$.)

$$A = \pi r^2 = (3.14)\left(\frac{0.17 \text{ cm}}{2}\right)^2 = 2.3 \times 10^{-2} \text{ cm}^2$$

3. **Organizing Data** Using the answers to Analysis items **1** and **2**, calculate the average number of tracks per cm^2.

$$\frac{5.3 \text{ tracks}}{0.023 \text{ cm}^2} = 230 \text{ tracks/cm}^2$$

Name _____ Class _____ Date _____

Detecting Radioactivity continued

4. Organizing Data In Analysis item **3** you calculated the number of tracks that accumulated per cm^2 over the total period the detector was in place. Divide this number by the number of days the detector was in place to calculate tracks/cm^2/day.

$$\frac{230 \text{ tracks/cm}^2}{24.19 \text{ days}} = 9.5 \text{ tracks/cm}^2/\text{day}$$

5. Organizing Data Several pieces of CR-39 plastic were sent to a facility that had a radon chamber in which the activity of the radon was known to be 13.69 Bq/L (becquerels per liter of air), as measured by a different technique. A becquerel is the name for the SI unit of activity for a radioactive substance and is equal to 1 decay/s. The exposed pieces of CR-39 plastic were etched, counted, and found to have an activity of 2370 tracks/cm^2/day. Calculate the radon activity measured by your detector in becquerels/liter. (Hint: Use the proportion 13.69 Bq/L:2370 tracks/cm^2/day as a conversion factor to convert your data.)

$$9.5 \text{ tracks/cm}^2/\text{day} \times \frac{13.69 \text{ Bq/L}}{2373 \text{ tracks/cm}^2/\text{day}} = 5.5 \times 10^{-2} \text{ Bq/L}$$

6. Relating Ideas The Environmental Protection Agency and other U.S. government agencies use non-SI units of picocuries per liter (pCi/L) to measure radiation. One curie is 3.7×10^{10} Bq, and one picocurie is 10^{-12} curies. Convert your data into units of pCi/L.

$$5.5 \times 10^{-2} \text{ Bq/L} \times \frac{1 \text{ Ci}}{3.7 \times 10^{10} \text{ Bq}} \times \frac{10^{12} \text{ pCi}}{1 \text{ Ci}} = 1.5 \text{ pCi/L}$$

7. Organizing Data Combine your data with those of other teams in your class, and jointly construct a map of your region that shows the levels of radon activity in Bq/L and pCi/L at various locations throughout your community.
Student answers will vary.

Name _____ Class _____ Date _____

Detecting Radioactivity *continued*

Conclusions

1. **Applying Ideas** The half-life of $^{222}_{86}$Rn is 3.823 days. After what time will only one-fourth of a given amount of radon remain?

   <u>One-fourth will remain after 2 half-lives, 7.646 days.</u>

2. **Designing Experiments** Factors other than geographic location can have an effect on radon emissions. For example, readings taken in basements are likely to be higher than those in attics. Design an experiment to test different aspects of the three highest and three lowest regions of radiation on the map to examine the influence of these other factors. If your teacher approves your suggestion, try it.

   <u>Students' suggestions will vary. Be sure that student plans meet all neces-</u>

   <u>sary safety guidelines before allowing students to try them.</u>

3. **Designing Experiments** CR-39 plastic could be used for further investigations of naturally occurring radiation. Design an experiment to explore one of the following areas. If your teacher approves your plan, carry out the experiment.

   • the range of alpha particles

   • the radon activity in soil

   • radioactivity of common items such as lantern mantles (Coleman green label), glow-in-the-dark clock or watch faces, and pieces of Fiestaware

   <u>Students' suggestions will vary. Be sure that student plans meet all neces-</u>

   <u>sary safety guidelines before allowing students to try them.</u>

Answer Key

Concept Review: Atomic Nuclei and Nuclear Stability

1. A nucleon is the protons and neutrons of a nucleus.
2. A nuclide is a general term applied to a specific nucleus with a given number of protons and neutrons.
3. The strong force is an attraction that exists between nucleons that is stronger than electrostatic repulsion between nucleons. This force is exerted when nucleons are very close to each other.
4. Nuclear binding energy is the energy released when nucleons come together.
5. The mass of any nucleus is less than the combined masses of its separated parts. The energy released when nucleons join results in this mass defect.
6. d
7. a
8. d
9. b
10. b
11. mass defect, mass, nucleus, mole, less, protons, nuclear binding, separate
12. increase, maximum, decrease, highest, large, attractions, repulsions, stable, $^{56}_{26}$Fe.
13. lower
14. large
15. mass
16. stability
17. more
18. equal to or greater than
19. 60%
20. stable
21. stable

Concept Review: Nuclear Change

1. Radioactivity is the process in which an unstable nucleus spontaneously changes to form a more stable one.

This change involves the release of particles, electromagnetic waves, or both.
2. If an isotope has too many neutrons, the nucleus will decay and emit radiation. A neutron may emit a high-energy electron, called a beta particle, and change to a proton. This process often occurs in unstable nuclei that have large N/Z numbers.
3. A nucleus that has too many protons can become stable by absorbing one of the atom's electrons. The nucleus releases gamma rays.
4. Some nuclei with too many protons emit positrons, or antiparticles of electrons. The proton is changed into a neutron.
5. An unstable nucleus with an N/Z number much larger than 1 can decay by emitting an alpha particle.

6.

Type of radioactive decay	What happens to atomic number?	What happens to mass number?
beta-particle emission	increases by one	does not change
electron capture	decreases by one	does not change
positron emission	decreases by one	does not change
alpha particle emission	decreases by two	decreases by four

7. $^{51}_{23}$V; gamma ray
8. $^{222}_{86}$Rn; alpha particle
9. $^{239}_{92}$U; positron
10. $^{234}_{92}$U; beta particle
11. $^{0}_{+1}e$; positron
12. $^{4}_{2}$He; alpha particle
13. $^{0}_{-1}e$; beta particle
14. annihilation of matter
15. positron emission

16. electron capture
17. alpha decay
18. beta emission
19. beta particles
20. antiparticle
21. electromagnetic radiation or gamma rays
22. Gamma
23. electron capture
24. neutron
25. alpha decay
26. alpha particle
27. 2, 4
28. fission, binding energy, spontaneous, neutrons, chain reaction, sustains, critical mass
29. fusion, fuse
30. fusion
31. fission
32. fission
33. fusion
34. **Benefits:** can produce a large amount of energy; one gram of uranium-235 generates as much energy as the combustion of 2700 kilograms of coal; only 100 reactors generate 20 percent of the electricity used in the United States.
    Hazards: chain reactions that occur in nuclear reactors can be very dangerous if they are not contained; radioactive wastes are generated.
35. Nuclear fusion occurs when small nuclei combine to form a larger, more stable nucleus. Energy is released as the new nucleus forms. It is not a practical energy source now because it takes a lot of energy and tremendous temperatures to start such a reaction. It is also hard to contain the reactants.

Concept Review: Uses of Nuclear Chemistry

1. The time required for half of a sample of a radioactive substance to disintegrate by radioactive decay or natural processes.

2. If we know the half-life of a radioactive isotope, we can then measure how much of the isotope is in an object and figure out how long the radioactive isotope has been decaying, which gives the age of the object.
3. b
4. d
5. a
6. a
7. a
8. a
9. b
10. a
11. c
12. b
13. c
14. Acute exposure to large doses of radiation over a short time can lead to radiation sickness and even death. Chronic exposure to low levels of radiation can be as dangerous as acute exposure and can lead to certain types of cancer.
15. All the reactions emit gamma rays, and all use radioactive isotopes with short half-lives.
16. 1 microgram , $\frac{1}{2}$ microgram; $\frac{1}{4}$ microgram, $\frac{1}{8}$ microgram
17. $\frac{1}{8}$
18. 8 grams
19. about 11 400 years
20. 6.25%

Answer Key

Quiz—Section: Atomic Nuclei and Nuclear Stability

1. b	6. d
2. a	7. b
3. b	8. c
4. c	9. c
5. d	10. b

Quiz—Section: Nuclear Change

1. b	6. c
2. b	7. d
3. c	8. a
4. d	9. d
5. c	10. c

Quiz—Section: Uses of Nuclear Chemistry

1. c	6. c
2. b	7. d
3. c	8. d
4. c	9. c
5. c	10. d

Chapter Test

1. c	11. b
2. b	12. c
3. b	13. c
4. b	14. d
5. a	15. d
6. a	16. b
7. b	17. c
8. b	18. d
9. d	19. c
10. d	20. d

21. The protons in the nucleus exert a repulsive electrostatic force on each other, tending to push the nucleus apart. The strong nuclear force holds the nucleons together. If there is an imbalance between the two forces, the nucleus will decay.

22. The product would be a nobelium-254 nucleus.

23. For nuclei smaller than iron-56 and nickel-58, the addition of nucleons lowers the energy of the nucleus because the short-range strong nuclear force is stronger than the electrostatic repulsion between protons. In nuclei larger than iron-56 and nickel-58, the electrostatic repulsion between protons is stronger than the nuclear force.

24. Two helium nuclei fuse and form beyllium-8 with the release of energy in the form of gamma rays.

25. $^{45}_{20}\text{Ca} \rightarrow \,^{45}_{21}\text{Sc} + \,^{0}_{-1}e$

Nuclear Chemistry

MULTIPLE CHOICE

1. In nuclear chemistry, a nucleon is a
   a. nuclide.
   b. neutron.
   c. proton.
   d. Both (b) and (c)

   Answer: D   Difficulty: I   Section: 1   Objective: 1

2. A nuclide is a
   a. nucleus of an atom with a specific number of protons.
   b. nucleus of an atom with a specific number of neutrons.
   c. nucleus of an atom with a specific number of protons and neutrons.
   d. free nucleon.

   Answer: C   Difficulty: I   Section: 1   Objective: 1

3. A nuclide is identified by which of the following?
   a. the number of protons in its nucleus
   b. the number of neutrons in its nucleus
   c. the number of protons and neutrons in its nucleus
   d. none of above

   Answer: C   Difficulty: I   Section: 1   Objective: 1

4. A nuclide is represented by which of the following?
   a. the symbol of the element preceded by a superscript indicating its mass number and a subscript indicating its atomic number
   b. the symbol of the element preceded by a superscript indicating its atomic number and a subscript indicating its mass number
   c. the full name of the element followed by a hyphen and the mass number
   d. Both (a) and (c)

   Answer: D   Difficulty: I   Section: 1   Objective: 1

5. Without the strong nuclear force, the nuclei of atoms would
   a. collapse.
   b. fly apart.
   c. gain electrons.
   d. double in size.

   Answer: B   Difficulty: I   Section: 1   Objective: 1

6 What does the 4 in $^{4}_{2}$He represent?
   a. the mass number
   b. the atomic number
   c. the number of protons
   d. the number of neutrons

   Answer: A   Difficulty: I   Section: 1   Objective: 1

7. What does the 101 in $^{256}_{101}$Md represent?
   a. the mass number
   b. the atomic number
   c. the nuclide number
   d. the number of neutrons

   Answer: B   Difficulty: I   Section: 1   Objective: 1

8. What does the 218 in polonium-218 represent?
   a. the mass number
   b. the atomic number
   c. the mass defect
   d. the neutron number

   Answer: A   Difficulty: I   Section: 1   Objective: 1

9. Mass defect is the difference between the
   a. mass of a nucleus and the mass of its atom.
   b. masses of a neutron and a proton.
   c. sum of the masses of the separate nucleons and the mass of the nuclide.
   d. masses of an atom and its electrons.

   Answer: C   Difficulty: I   Section:1   Objective: 2

10. Which of the following is the correct relationship between mass and energy?
    a. $E = mc^2$ c. $E^2 = mc$
    b. $E = mc$ d. $E = m^2c$

    Answer: A   Difficulty: I   Section: 1   Objective: 2

11. The nuclear binding energy is released when a nucleus
    a. is bombarded.   c. is formed from its constituent particles.
    b. divides.   d. decays.

    Answer: C   Difficulty: I   Section: 1   Objective: 2

12. Elements with the greatest nuclear binding energies per nuclear particle are the
    a. smallest in size.   c. most stable.
    b. least stable.   d. largest in size.

    Answer: C   Difficulty: I   Section: 1   Objective: 2

13. Compared with the sum of the masses of the separate particles that compose the nucleus, the mass of the nucleus
    a. is always less.   c. is always the same.
    b. is always more.   d. may be either less, more, or the same.

    Answer: A   Difficulty: I   Section: 1   Objective: 2

14. Between protons in a nucleus,
    a. attraction due to nuclear force is greater than repulsion due to electrostatic force.
    b. repulsion due to electrostatic force is greater than attraction due to nuclear force.
    c. nuclear and electrostatic forces are balanced.
    d. electrostatic forces are negligible.

    Answer: A   Difficulty: I   Section: 1   Objective: 2

15. Among atoms with low atomic numbers, what is the neutron-proton ratio of the most stable nuclei?
    a. 1.8   c. 1.0
    b. 1.5   d. 0.5

    Answer: C   Difficulty: I   Section: 1   Objective: 3

16. The number of each type of nucleon in a stable nucleus is commonly
    a. even.   c. not a whole number.
    b. odd.   d. a magic number.

    Answer: A   Difficulty: I   Section: 1   Objective: 3

17. Why are 2, 8, 20, 28, 50, and 82 considered "magic numbers" in a nuclide?
    a. These numbers represent the mass numbers of a stable nuclides.
    b. These numbers represent the number of protons in stable nuclides.
    c. These numbers represent the number of neutrons in stable nuclides.
    d. Both (b) and (c)

    Answer: D   Difficulty: I   Section: 1   Objective: 3

18. In a nuclear reaction, unstable nuclei that change their number of protons and neutrons,
    a. give off large amounts of energy, and increase their stability.
    b. give off small amounts of energy, and increase their stability.
    c. give off large amounts of energy, and decrease their stability.
    d. give off small amounts of energy, and decrease their stability.

    Answer: A   Difficulty: I   Section: 1   Objective: 3

19. The energy released in a nuclear reaction comes from
    a. electrons.
    b. bonds.
    c. positrons.
    d. the binding energy of the nucleus.

    Answer: D   Difficulty: I   Section: 1   Objective: 3

20. Which of the following lists ranks nuclear radiation from most massive to least massive?
    a. alpha, beta, gamma
    b. beta, gamma, alpha
    c. gamma, alpha, beta
    d. gamma, beta, alpha

    Answer: A   Difficulty: I   Section: 2   Objective: 1

21. Which of the following particles has the same mass as an electron but a positive charge and is sometimes emitted from the nucleus during radioactive decay?
    a. beta particle
    b. alpha particle
    c. positron
    d. gamma ray

    Answer: C   Difficulty: I   Section: 2   Objective: 1

22. Which series consists of radioactive nuclides produced by successive radioactive decay until a stable nuclide is reached?
    a. parent series
    b. half-life series
    c. nuclide series
    d. decay series

    Answer: D   Difficulty: I   Section: 2   Objective: 1

23. Of the following reactions, which is a fission reaction?
    a. hydrogen-2 and hydrogen-3 combining to form a helium-4 atom and a neutron
    b. carbon-12 and hydrogen-1 combining to form a nitrogen-13 atom
    c. uranium-235 absorbing a neutron and splitting into barium-141, krypton-92, and three neutrons
    d. a glucose molecule being metabolized with oxygen into carbon dioxide and water

    Answer: C   Difficulty: I   Section: 2   Objective: 2

24. Reaction _____ in the figure shown is an example of a fission reaction.

a.
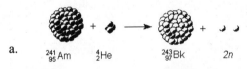

b.

c.

d.
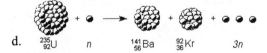

    Answer: D   Difficulty: I   Section: 2   Objective: 2

25. If the particle that starts a nuclear reaction is also one of the products, the process is a
    a. chain reaction.
    b. neutron emission.
    c. nuclear fusion.
    d. neutron bombardment.

    Answer: A   Difficulty: I   Section: 2   Objective: 2

26. Of the following reactions, which is a fusion reaction?
    a. uranium-235 absorbing a neutron and splitting into xenon-140, strontium-94, and two neutrons
    b. hydrochloric acid combining with sodium hydroxide to form a salt and water
    c. carbon-14 decaying into nitrogen-14 and a beta particle
    d. curium-246 combining with carbon-12 to form nobelium-254 and four neutrons
    Answer: D   Difficulty: I   Section: 2   Objective: 3

27. Which statement about nuclear reactions is NOT true?
    a. Nuclear power plants use fission of uranium.
    b. In fission, the total mass of the reactants equals the total mass of the products.
    c. In fission, nuclei are split, and in fusion, nuclei are combined.
    d. Energy as heat and light in the sun are generated by hydrogen fusion reactions.
    Answer: B   Difficulty: I   Section: 2   Objective: 3

28. The half-life of an isotope is the time required for half the nuclei in a sample of the isotope to
    a. undergo radioactive decay.   c. undergo nuclear fusion.
    b. undergo nuclear fission.   d. react chemically.
    Answer: A   Difficulty: I   Section: 3   Objective: 1

29. Which statement is true about half-lives?
    a. Different atoms of the same nuclide have different half-lives.
    b. Each radioactive nuclide has its own half-life.
    c. All radioactive nuclides of an element have the same half-life.
    d. All radioactive nuclides have the same half-life.
    Answer: B   Difficulty: I   Section: 3   Objective: 1

30. How many half-lives are required for three-fourths of the nuclei of an isotope in a sample to decay?
    a. $\dfrac{3}{4}$ c. 2

    b. $\dfrac{3}{2}$ d. 3
    Answer: C   Difficulty: I   Section: 3   Objective: 1

31. What is the half-life of an isotope if 125 g of a 500 g sample of the isotope remains after 3.0 years?
    a. 1.5 years   c. 3.5 years
    b. 2.5 years   d. 4.5 years
    Answer: A   Difficulty: III   Section: 3   Objective: 1

32. To use radioactive dating for a substance, you must know the substance's
    a. melting point.   c. rate of weathering or erosion.
    b. half-life.   d. heat of reaction.
    Answer: B   Difficulty: I   Section: 3   Objective: 1

Table 1 Half-Lives of Several Radioactive Nuclides

Nuclide	Half-life (years)
carbon-14	5.71×10^3
potassium-40	1.26×10^9
radium-226	1.60×10^3
thorium-230	7.54×10^4
uranium-235	7.04×10^8

33. According to Table 1, the appropriate radioactive isotope to use to estimate the age of a rock from a rock formation believed to be a billion years old is
    a. carbon-14.
    b. potassium-40.
    c. radium-226.
    d. thorium-230.

    Answer: B   Difficulty: II   Section: 3   Objective: 1

34. According to Table 1, if a rock contains 25% as much uranium-235 as rocks being formed today, how old is the rock?
    a. 7.04×10^8 years
    b. 3.55×10^8 years
    c. 2.84×10^9 years
    d. 1.41×10^9 years

    Answer: D   Difficulty: III   Section: 3   Objective: 1

35. Balance the following equation: $^{226}_{88}\text{Ra} \rightarrow \,^{222}_{86}\text{Rn}^+$ _____.

    a. ^4_2He
    b. ^1_0n
    c. ^1_1H
    d. $^0_{-1}\text{e}$

    Answer: A   Difficulty: II   Section: 2   Objective: 1

36. What unit is used to measure radiation damage to human tissue?
    a. roentgen
    b. rem
    c. rad
    d. half-life

    Answer: B   Difficulty: I   Section: 3   Objective: 3

37. How do radioactive nuclides affect photographic film wrapped in lightproof paper?
    a. They have no effect on the film.
    b. They disintegrate the film.
    c. They melt the film.
    d. They fog the film.

    Answer: D   Difficulty: I   Section: 3   Objective: 3

COMPLETION

38. A nucleon is a proton or a(n) _____.

    Answer: neutron   Difficulty: I   Section: 1   Objective: 1

39. A nucleus of an atom with a specific number of protons and neutrons is called a(n)

    _____.

    Answer: nuclide   Difficulty: I   Section: 1   Objective: 1

40. Nuclides that have the same atomic number but different mass numbers are classified as

    _____.

    Answer: isotopes   Difficulty: I   Section: 1   Objective: 1

41. The nuclide $^{125}_{53}\text{I}$ contains _____ protons.

    Answer: 53   Difficulty: I   Section: 1   Objective: 1

42. The nuclide $^{197}_{79}Au$ contains _____ neutrons.

    Answer: 118   Difficulty: I   Section: 1   Objective: 1

43. The interaction that binds nucleons together in a nucleus is called the _____.

    Answer: strong force   Difficulty: I   Section: 1   Objective: 2

44. The difference between the sum of the individual masses of the protons, neutrons, and electrons in an atom and the mass of the atom is called _____ .

    Answer: mass defect   Difficulty: I   Section: 1   Objective: 2

45. The range of neutron/protons ratios of stable nuclei has a minimum numerical value of 1.0 and a maximum numerical value of _____.

    Answer: 1.5   Difficulty: I   Section: 1   Objective: 3

46. The largest stable nucleus has an atomic number of _____.

    Answer: 83   Difficulty: I   Section: 1   Objective: 3

47. The process by which an unstable nucleus emits one or more particles, or energy in the form of electromagnetic radiation is called _____.

    Answer: radioactivity   Difficulty: I   Section: 2   Objective: 1

48. The symbol, ^4_2He, represents a(n) _____ particle.

    Answer: alpha   Difficulty: I   Section: 2   Objective: 1

49. The symbol, $^0_{-1}e$, represents a(n) _____ particle.

    Answer: beta   Difficulty: I   Section: 2   Objective: 1

50. In an alpha decay, the number of _____ and the number of _____ are each reduced by two in a nuclide.

    Answer: protons; neutrons

    Difficulty: II   Section: 2   Objective: 2

51. In a positron emission, the number of _____ increases by one and the number of _____ decreases one in a nuclide.

    Answer: neutrons, protons

    Difficulty: II   Section: 2   Objective: 2

52. The combination of the nuclei of small atoms to form a larger nucleus is called nuclear _____.

    Answer: fusion   Difficulty: I   Section: 2   Objective: 2

53. The critical mass is the minimum mass of a fissionable isotope that provides the number of neutrons needed to sustain a(n) _____.

    Answer: chain reaction

    Difficulty: I   Section: 2   Objective:2

54. The splitting of the nucleus of a large atom into two or more fragments is called nuclear _____.

    Answer: fission   Difficulty: I   Section: 2   Objective: 3

55. Stars, including our sun, generate energy in the process called nuclear _____.

    Answer: fusion   Difficulty: I   Section: 2   Objective: 3

56. Smoke detectors use the ionization properties of a type of nuclear decay called _____ decay to detect changes in air caused by smoke particles.

    Answer: alpha   Difficulty: I   Section: 3   Objective: 2

57. The curie is the unit in which radioactive decay is measured; the unit that is used to measure the biological effect of the absorbed dose of radiation in humans is the _____.

Answer: rem   Difficulty: I   Section: 3   Objective: 3

58. Nuclear _____ is "spent fuel" that can no longer be used to create energy.

Answer: waste   Difficulty: I   Section: 3   Objective: 3

59. To monitor the approximate radiation exposure of people working with radioactive materials _____ are often worn by the workers.

Answer: film badges   Difficulty: I   Section: 3   Objective: 3

SHORT ANSWER

60. How does the strong nuclear force stabilize the nucleus?
Answer: The strong nuclear force counteracts the electrostatic repulsion forces within the nucleus.
Difficulty: I   Section: 1   Objective: 1

61. Where does the binding energy come from?
Answer: Binding energy comes from the mass defect of the nucleus.
Difficulty: I   Section: 1   Objective: 2

62. Explain why the nucleus is at a lower energy than its separated nucleons.
Answer: Energy is given off when the nucleons come within a small distance of one another, and the strong nuclear force of attraction keeps the nuclear particles close together.
Difficulty: II   Section: 1   Objective: 2

63. Briefly describe alpha particles, beta particles, and gamma rays.
Answer: Alpha particles are helium nuclei that are emitted from heavy elements. Beta particles are high-energy electrons emitted from nuclei when neutrons become protons. Gamma rays are high-energy electromagnetic waves.
Difficulty: II   Section: 2   Objective: 1

64. Explain how a chain reaction is sustained.
Answer: Neutrons that are the products of a nuclear reaction can initiate the same nuclear reaction in surrounding materials, producing more neutrons to initiate more reactions.
Difficulty: II   Section: 2   Objective: 3

65. Why do elements such as radium, polonium, and uranium expose photographic film
Answer: All of these elements give off energy in the form of radiation.
Difficulty: II   Section: 3   Objective: 3

ESSAY QUESTIONS

66. Use the concepts of electrostatic force and strong force to explain why some atoms decay.
Answer: The protons in a nucleus exert a repulsive electric force on each other, tending to push the nucleus apart. The strong nuclear force holds the nucleons together. If there is an imbalance between the two forces, the nucleus will decay.
Difficulty: II   Section: 1   Objective: 1

67. Describe the origin of binding energy and its relationship to the Einstein mass-energy equation.
Answer: When protons and neutrons form a nucleus, energy is released. This energy is called the nuclear binding energy. This energy comes from the conversion of a small amount of mass into energy. The amount of energy is determined from the equation $E = mc^2$.
Difficulty: II   Section: 1   Objective: 2

68. What happens if there are too many or too few neutrons in a nucleus?

Answer: When there are too few neutrons, the electrostatic repulsion outweighs the strong nuclear force, and the atom decays. When there are too many neutrons, the nucleus becomes too large and unstable.

Difficulty: II   Section: 1   Objective: 3

69. Compare nuclear fission and nuclear fusion.

Answer: Both change one element into another by changing the number of protons in the nucleus and release energy. Nuclear fusion is the combining of two or more nuclei. Nuclear fission is the splitting of a nucleus into smaller nuclei.

Difficulty: II   Section: 2   Objective: 3

70. Explain the process of radioactive dating.

Answer: The radioactive isotopes in a material decay over time. If the half-life of an isotope and the original amount of the isotope are known, the age of the material containing the isotope can be estimated.

Difficulty: II   Section: 3   Objective: 1

PROBLEMS

71. Calculate the mass defect and the binding energy/nucleon of the nuclide $^{9}_{4}Be$ which has a mass of 9.012 182 24 amu. The mass of a proton is 1.007 276 47 amu and the mass of a neutron is 1.008 664 90. One amu = 1.6605×10^{-27} kg and the speed of light is 3.00×10^{8} m/s.
Answer:

mass defect = 4(mass of proton) + 5(mass of neutron) − mass of nuclide

$\quad\quad\quad$ = 4(1.007 276 47 amu) +5(1.008 664 90 amu) − 9.012 182 24 amu

$\quad\quad\quad$ = 4.029 105 88 amu + 5.043 324 50 amu −9.012 182 24 amu

$\quad\quad\quad$ = 9.072 130 38 amu − 9.012 182 24 amu

mass defect = 0.059 948 14 amu

binding energy/nucleon = $(0.59\ 984\ 14\ \text{amu})(1.6605 \times 10^{-27}\ \text{kg/amu})(3 \times 10^{8}\ \text{m/s})^{2}$/9 nucleons

$\quad\quad\quad\quad\quad$ = 8.96×10^{-11} J/9

binding energy/nucleon = 9.66×10^{-12} J/nucleon

Difficulty: III   Section: 1   Objective: 2

72. Write the nuclear equation for each of the following reactions. Refer to a periodic table.

a. the alpha decay of $^{226}_{88}Ra$

Answer:

$\quad ^{226}_{88}Ra \rightarrow\ ^{4}_{2}He +\ ^{222}_{86}Rn$

Difficulty: II   Section: 2   Objective: 1

b. the beta decay of $^{39}_{17}Cl$

Answer:

$\quad ^{39}_{17}Cl \rightarrow\ ^{0}_{-1}e +\ ^{39}_{18}Ar$

Difficulty: II   Section: 2   Objective: 1

c. the positron emission of $^{30}_{15}P$

Answer:

$\quad ^{30}_{15}P \rightarrow\ ^{0}_{-1}e +\ ^{30}_{14}Si$

Difficulty: II   Section: 2   Objective: 1

Solutions Manual

Solutions for problems can also be found at go.hrw.com. Enter the keyword HW4NUCTNS to obtain solutions.

Practice Problems A

1. Given: $^{218}_{89}Po \rightarrow ^4_2He + ?$

mass number: $218 - 4 = 214$

atomic number: $84 - 2 = 82$

$? = ^{214}_{82}Pb$

2. Given: $^{142}_{61}Pm + ? \rightarrow ^{142}_{60}Nd$

mass number: $142 - 142 = 0$

atomic number: $60 - 61 = -1$

$? = ^0_{-1}e$

3. Given: $^{253}_{99}Es + ^4_2He \rightarrow ^1_0n + ?$

mass number: $253 + 4 - 1 = 256$

atomic number: $99 + 2 - 0 = 101$

$? = ^{256}_{101}Md$

Section 2 Review

5. a. Given: $^{233}_{92}U \rightarrow ^4_2He + ?$

mass number: $233 - 4 = 229$

atomic number: $92 - 2 = 90$

$? = ^{229}_{90}Th$

b. Given: $^{66}_{29}Cu + ^0_{-1}e \rightarrow ?$

mass number: $66 + 0 = 66$

atomic number: $= 29 + (-1) = 28$

$? = ^{66}_{28}Ni$

c. Given: $^9_4Be + ^4_2He \rightarrow ^{13}_6C$

$^{13}_6C \rightarrow ^1_0n + ?$

mass number: $13 - 1 = 12$

atomic number: $6 - 0 = 6$

$? = ^{12}_6C$

d. Given: $^{238}_{92}U + ^1_0n \rightarrow ?$

$? \rightarrow 2^0_{-1}\beta + ^{239}_{94}Pu$

mass number: $238 + 1 = 239$

atomic number: $92 + 0 = 92$

$? = ^{239}_{92}U$

6. Given: $2\left(^3_2He\right) \rightarrow 2\left(^1_1H\right) + ?$

mass number: $[2(3) - 2(1)] = 6 - 2 = 4$

atomic number: $[2(2) - 2(1)] = 4 - 2 = 2$

$? = ^4_2He$

| Solutions Manual *continued*

Practice Problems B

1. Given: half-life of radium-226 = 1599 years

Unknown: number of years needed for decay of $\frac{15}{16}$ of a given amount of radium-226

amount remaining $= \frac{1}{16} = 0.0625 = \left(\frac{1}{2}\right)^4$; 4 half-lives

years needed for decay of $\frac{15}{16} = (1599 \text{ years})(4) = 6396$ years

2. Given: half-life of radon-222 = 3.824 days

Unknown: time needed for $\frac{1}{4}$ of a given amount of radon-222 to remain

number of half-lives: $\left(\frac{1}{4}\right) = 0.25 = \left(\frac{1}{2}\right)^2$; 2 half-lives

days needed for $\frac{3}{4}$ to decay $= (3.284 \text{ days})(2) = 7.648$ days

3. Given: half-life of polonium-218 = 3.0 min starting mass of polonium-218 = 16 mg

Unknown: length of time before 1.0 mg of polonium-218 remains

amount remaining $= \left(\frac{1}{16}\right) = 0.0625 = \left(\frac{1}{2}\right)^4$; 4 half-lives

time until 1.0 mg remains $= (3.0 \text{ min})(4) = 12$ min

Practice Problems C

1. Given: orig. mass of $^{210}\text{Po} = 2.0$ mg half-life of ^{210}Po = 138.4 days time elapsed = 415.2 days

Unknown: mass of ^{210}Po remaining after 415.2 days

number of half-lives: $(415.2 \text{ days})\left(\dfrac{1 \text{ half-life}}{138.4 \text{ days}}\right) = 3$ half-lives

mass of ^{210}Po remaining $= (2.0 \text{ mg})\left(\dfrac{1}{2}\right)^3 = 0.25$ mg

2. Given: half-life of ^{226}Ra = 1599 years orig. mass of ^{226}Ra = 0.250 g

Unknown: mass remaining after 4797 years

number of half-lives $= (4797 \text{ years})\left(\dfrac{1 \text{ half-life}}{1599 \text{ years}}\right) = 3$ half-lives

mass remaining $= (0.0250 \text{ g})\left(\dfrac{1}{2}\right)^3 = 0.0312$ g

3. Given: half-life of radium-224 = 3.66 days

mass remaining after 7.32 days = 0.0800 g

Unknown: original mass of radium-224

number of half-lives = $(7.32 \text{ days})\left(\dfrac{1 \text{ half-life}}{3.66 \text{ days}}\right)$ = 2 half-lives

x = original mass

$(x)\left(\dfrac{1}{2}\right)^2 = 0.0800 \text{ g}$

$x = (0.0800 \text{ g})\left(\dfrac{2}{1}\right)^2 = 0.32 \text{ g}$

Section 3 Review

5. Given: radioactive isotope

Unknown: fraction of original sample remaining after 3 half-lives

fraction remaining = $\left(\dfrac{1}{2}\right)^3 = \dfrac{1}{8}$

6. Given: mass remaining of radon-222 = 5.2 × 10^{-8} g

time elapsed = 11.46

Unknown: number of half-lives passed original mass of ^{222}Rn

half-life of ^{222}Rn = 3.82 days

number of half-lives = $(11.46 \text{ days})\left(\dfrac{1 \text{ half-life}}{3.82 \text{ days}}\right)$ = 3 half-lives

x = original mass

$x\left(\dfrac{1}{2}\right)^3 = 5.2 \times 10^{-8} \text{ g}$

$x = (5.2 \times 10^{-8} \text{ g})\left(\dfrac{2}{1}\right)^3$

$\quad = 4.16 \times 10^{-7}$

7. Given: half-life of protactinium-234 = 6.69 h

Unknown: fraction remaining after 26.76 h

number of half-lives = $(26.76 \text{ h})\left(\dfrac{1 \text{ half-life}}{6.69 \text{ h}}\right)$ = 4 half-lives

fraction remaining after 4 half-lives = $\left(\dfrac{1}{2}\right)^4 = \dfrac{1}{16}$

8. Given: half-life of thorium-227 = 18.72 days

Unknown: length of time for $\frac{3}{4}$ of a given amount to decay

amount remaining = $\dfrac{1}{4} = \left(\dfrac{1}{2}\right)^2$; 2 half-lives

length of time for decay = $(18.72 \text{ days})(2) = 37.44 \text{ days}$

Chapter Review

30. Given: $^{238}_{92}U \rightarrow ^4_2He + ?$ mass number: $238 - 4 = 234$

atomic number: $92 - 2 = 90$

$? = ^{234}_{90}Th$

$^{238}_{92}U \rightarrow ^4_2He + ^{234}_{90}Th$

31. Given: $^{43}_{19}K \rightarrow ^{43}_{20}Ca + ?$ mass number: $43 - 43 = 0$

Unknown: nuclear equation   atomic number: $19 - 20 = -1$

$? = ^0_{-1}e$

32. Given: $^{222}_{86}Rn \rightarrow ^4_2He + ?$ mass number: $224 - 4 = 220$

Unknown: nuclear equation   atomic number: $= 86 - 2 = 84$

$? = ^{220}_{84}Po$

$^{222}_{84}Rn \rightarrow ^4_2He + ^{220}_{84}Po$

33. Given: $^{235}_{92}U \rightarrow ^4_2He + a$
$a \rightarrow ^0_{-1}e + b$
$b \rightarrow ^4_2He + c$
$c \rightarrow ^0_{-1}e + d$
$d \rightarrow ^4_2He + f$
$f \rightarrow ^4_2He + g$
$g \rightarrow ^4_2He + h$
$h \rightarrow ^4_2He + j$
$j \rightarrow ^0_{-1}e + k$
$k \rightarrow ^0_{-1}e + l$
$l \rightarrow ^4_2He + ^{207}_{82}Pb$

Unknown: a-l

a: mass number: $235 - 4 = 231$

atomic number: $92 - 2 = 90$

$a = ^{231}_{90}Th$

$^{235}_{92}U \rightarrow ^{231}_{90}Th + ^4_2He$

b: mass number: $231 - 0 = 231$

atomic number: $90 - (-1) = 91$

$b = ^{231}_{91}Pa$

$^{231}_{90}Th \rightarrow ^{231}_{91}Pa + ^0_{-1}e$

c: mass number: $231 - 4 = 227$

atomic number: $91 - 2 = 89$

$c = ^{227}_{89}Ac$

$^{231}_{91}Pa \rightarrow ^{227}_{89}Ac + ^4_2He$

d: mass number: $227 - 0 = 227$

atomic number: $89 - (-1) = 90$

$d = ^{227}_{90}Th$

$^{227}_{89}Ac \rightarrow ^{227}_{90}Tn + ^0_{-1}e$

e: mass number: $227 - 4 = 223$

atomic number: $90 - 2 = 88$

$e = ^{223}_{88}Ra$

$^{227}_{90}Tn \rightarrow ^{223}_{88}Ra + ^4_2He$

Solutions Manual *continued*

f: mass number: $223 - 4 = 219$

atomic number: $88 - 2 = 86$

$f = {}^{219}_{86}\text{Rn}$

$${}^{223}_{88}\text{Ra} \rightarrow {}^{219}_{86}\text{Rn} + {}^{4}_{2}\text{He}$$

g: mass number: $219 - 4 = 215$

atomic number: $86 - 2 = 84$

$g = {}^{215}_{84}\text{Po}$

$${}^{219}_{86}\text{Rn} \rightarrow {}^{215}_{84}\text{Po} + {}^{4}_{2}\text{He}$$

h: mass number: $215 - 4 = 211$

atomic number: $84 - 2 = 82$

$h = {}^{211}_{82}\text{Pb}$

$${}^{215}_{84}\text{Po} \rightarrow {}^{211}_{82}\text{Pb} + {}^{4}_{2}\text{He}$$

i: mass number: $211 - 0 = 211$

atomic number: $82 - (-1) = 83$

$i = {}^{211}_{83}\text{Bi}$

$${}^{211}_{82}\text{Pb} \rightarrow {}^{211}_{83}\text{Bi} + {}^{0}_{-1}e$$

j: mass number: $211 - 0 = 211$

atomic number: $83 - (-1) = 84$

$j = {}^{211}_{84}\text{Po}$

$${}^{211}_{83}\text{Bi} \rightarrow {}^{211}_{84}\text{Po} + {}^{0}_{-1}e$$

k: mass number: $211 - 207 = 4$

atomic number: $84 - 2 = 82$

$k = {}^{207}_{82}\text{Pb}$

$${}^{211}_{84}\text{Bi} \rightarrow {}^{207}_{82}\text{Pb} + {}^{4}_{2}\text{He}$$

34. Given: a. $^{239}_{93}\text{Np} \rightarrow ^{0}_{-1}\beta + ?$
b. $^{9}_{4}\text{Be} + ^{4}_{2}\text{He} \rightarrow ?$
c. $^{32}_{15}\text{P} + ? \rightarrow ^{33}_{15}\text{P}$
d. $^{236}_{92}\text{U} \rightarrow ^{94}_{36}\text{Kr} + ? + 3^{1}_{0}n$

a. mass number: $239 - 0 = 239$

atomic number: $93 - (-1) = 94$

$? = ^{239}_{94}\text{Pu}$

b. mass number: $9 + 4 = 13$

atomic number: $4 + 2 = 6$

$? = ^{13}_{6}\text{C}$

c. mass number: $33 - 32 = 1$

atomic number: $15 - 15 = 0$

$? = ^{1}_{0}n$

d. mass number: $236 - 94 - 3 = 139$

atomic number: $92 - 36 - 0 = 56$

$? = ^{139}_{56}\text{Ba}$

---

37. Given: orig. mass of
copper-64 =
26.00 g
mass remaining
after 64 hours =
0.8125 g

Unknown: half-life of
copper-64

number of half-lives : $(26.00 \text{ g})\left(\frac{1}{2}\right)^{n} = 0.8125 \text{ g}$

$$\left(\frac{1}{2}\right)^{n} = \frac{0.8125 \text{ g}}{26.00 \text{ g}}$$

$$\log\left(\frac{1}{2}\right)^{n} = \log\left(\frac{0.8125}{26.00}\right)$$

$$n \log\left(\frac{1}{2}\right) = \log(0.03125)$$

$$n = \frac{\log(0.03125)}{\log(0.5)} = 5$$

$$\text{half-life} = \frac{64 \text{ hours}}{5 \text{ half-lives}} = 12.8 \text{ hours/half-life}$$

---

38. Given: half-life of
thorium-234 =
24.10 days

Unknown: length of
time for $\frac{15}{16}$
of 52.0 g of
thorium-234
to decay

amount remaining $= \frac{1}{16} = 0.0625 = \left(\frac{1}{2}\right)^{4}$; 4 half-lives

length of time for $\frac{15}{16}$ to decay $= 4(24.10 \text{ days}) = 96.4 \text{ days}$

---

41. Given: half-life of
radon-222 =
3.8 days
starting mass of
radon-222 = 4.38 g

Unknown: amount
remaining
after 15.2 days

number of half-lives $= (15.2 \text{ days})\left(\frac{1 \text{ half-life}}{3.8 \text{ days}}\right) = 4$ half-lives

mass remaining $= \left(\frac{1}{2}\right)^{4}(4.38 \text{ g}) = 0.274 \text{ g}$

Solutions Manual *continued*

42. Given: starting mass of phosphorus-32 = 10.0 mg

half-life of phosphorus-32 = 14.3 days

Unknown: mass remaining after 57 days

number of half-lives = $(57 \text{ days})\left(\dfrac{1 \text{ half-life}}{14.3 \text{ days}}\right) = 4$ half-lives

mass remaining = $\left(\dfrac{1}{2}\right)^4 (10.0 \text{ mg}) = 0.625$ mg

43. Given: orig. mass of $^{226}\text{Ra} = 0.250$ g

half-life of $^{226}\text{Ra} = 1599$ years

Unknown: mass remaining after 4797 years

number of half-lives = $(4797 \text{ years})\left(\dfrac{1 \text{ half-life}}{1599 \text{ years}}\right) = 3$ half-lives

mass remaining = $(0.450 \text{ g})\left(\dfrac{1}{2}\right)^3 = 0.056$ g

45. Given: a. $^{235}_{92}\text{U}$
b. $^{16}_{8}\text{O}$
c. $^{56}_{26}\text{Fe}$
d. $^{156}_{20}\text{Nd}$

Unknown: neutron-proton ratio

a. $^{235}_{92}\text{U}$ = 92 protons, 143 neutrons

$$\text{Ratio} = \frac{143}{92} = 1.55:1$$

b. $^{16}_{8}\text{O}$ = 8 protons, 8 neutrons

$$\text{Ratio} = \frac{8}{8} = 1:1$$

c. $^{56}_{26}\text{Fe}$ = 26 protons, 30 neutrons

$$\text{Ratio} = \frac{30}{26} = 1.15:1$$

d. $^{156}_{60}\text{Nd}$ = 60 protons, 96 neutrons

$$\text{Ratio} = \frac{96}{60} = 1.6:1$$

46. Given: atomic mass of $^{238}_{92}\text{U} = 238.050\ 784$ amu

Unknown: binding energy

number of neutrons = 238 − 92 = 146

$^{238}_{92}\text{U}$ = 92(1.007276 47 amu) + 146(1.008 664 90 amu)

= 239.9345 106 amu

mass defect = (239.9345 106 amu) − (238.050 784 amu)

= 1.883 726 64 amu

binding energy: $E = mc^2$

= [(1.883 726 64 amu)(1.6605 × 10^{-27} kg/amu)]

(3.00 × 10^8 m/s)^2

= 2.81 × 10^{-10} J

47. Given: binding energy
for $^{56}_{26}$Fe = 7.89 ×
10^{-11} J

Unknown: mass lost

$E = mc^2$

$m = \dfrac{E}{c^2}$

$= \dfrac{7.89 \times 10^{-11}(\text{kg} \cdot \text{m}^2/\text{s}^2)}{(3.00 \times 10^8 (\text{m/s})^2}$

$= 8.77 \times 10^{-28}$ kg

48. Given: measured atomic
mass of $^2_1$H =
2.0140 amu

Unknown: binding energy
for 1 mol of
deuterium
atoms

$^2_1$H = 1(1.007276 47 amu) + 1(1.008664 90 amu) = 2.01594 137 amu

mass defect = 2.01594 137 amu − 2.0140 amu = 1.9414×10^{-3} amu

binding energy: $E = mc^2$

$= (1.9414 \times 10^{-3} \text{ amu})(1.6605 \times 10^{-27} \text{ kg/amu})$

$(3.00 \times 10^8 \text{ m/s})^2$

$= 2.90 \times 10^{-13}$ J

binding energy/mol = $(2.90 \times 10^{-13} \text{ J/atom})(6.022 \times 10^{23} \text{ atoms/mol})$

$= 1.75 \times 10^{11}$ J/mol

50. Given: iodine-131

Unknown: nuclear
equation for
beta emission

$^{131}_{53}\text{I} \rightarrow {}^{131}_{54}\text{Xe} + {}^{0}_{-1}e$

52. Given: $^{232}_{90}$Th

Unknown: nuclear
equations
for alpha
emission,
beta emission,
beta emission,
and alpha
emission

$^{232}_{90}\text{Th} \rightarrow {}^{4}_{2}\text{He} + {}^{228}_{88}\text{Ra}$

$^{228}_{88}\text{Ra} \rightarrow {}^{0}_{-1}e + {}^{228}_{89}\text{Ac}$

$^{228}_{89}\text{Ac} \rightarrow {}^{0}_{-1}e + {}^{228}_{90}\text{Th}$

$^{228}_{90}\text{Th} \rightarrow {}^{4}_{2}\text{He} + {}^{224}_{88}\text{Ra}$

53. Given: half-life of
radium-224 =
3.66 days
mass remaining
after 7.32 days =
0.0500 g

Unknown: orig. mass of
radium-224

number of half-lives = $(7.32 \text{ days})\left(\dfrac{1 \text{ half-life}}{3.66 \text{ days}}\right) = 2$ half-lives

x = original mass

$x = \left(\dfrac{1}{2}\right)^2 = 0.0500$ g

$x = (0.0500 \text{ g})\left(\dfrac{2}{1}\right)^2 = 0.200$ g

54. Given: orig. mass of
radium-226 =
15.0 mg
half-life of
radium-226 =
1599 years

Unknown: mass
remaining
after 6396
year

number of half-lives = $(6396 \text{ years})\left(\dfrac{1 \text{ half-life}}{1599 \text{ years}}\right) = 4$ half-lives

mass remaining = $(15.0 \text{ mg})\left(\dfrac{1}{2}\right)^4 = 0.938$ mg

Standardized Test Prep

7. Given: $^{246}_{96}\text{Cm} + ^{12}_{6}\text{C} \rightarrow$?   mass number: $246 + 12 = 258$

atomic number: $96 + 6 = 102$

$? = ^{258}_{102}\text{No}$

8. Given: half-live of thorium-234 = 24 days starting mass of thorium-234 = 42.0 g

number of half-lives $= (72 \text{ days})\left(\dfrac{1 \text{ half-life}}{24 \text{ days}}\right) = 3$ half-lives

mass remaining $= (42.0 \text{ g})\left(\dfrac{1}{2}\right)^{3} = 5.25$ g

Unknown: mass remaining after 72 days

Problem Bank

1. Given: measured atomic mass of $^{20}_{10}\text{Ne} =$ 19.992 44 amu

10 protons: $(10 \times 1.007\ 276 \text{ amu})$

$= 10.072\ 76$ amu

Unknown: mass defect

10 neutrons: $(10 \times 1.008\ 665 \text{ amu})$

$= 10.086\ 65$ amu

10 electrons: $(10 \times 0.000\ 5486 \text{ amu})$

$= 0.005\ 486$ amu

total combined mass: 20.164 896 amu

mass defect

$= 20.164\ 896 \text{ amu} - 19.992\ 44 \text{ amu}$

$= 0.172\ 46$ amu

2. Given: measured atomic mass of $^{7}_{3}\text{Li} =$ 7.016 00 amu

3 protons: $(3 \times 1.007\ 276 \text{ amu})$

$= 3.021\ 828$ amu

Unknown: mass defect

4 neutrons: $(4 \times 1.008\ 665 \text{ amu})$

$= 4.034\ 66$ amu

3 electrons: $(3 \times 0.000\ 5486 \text{ amu})$

$= 0.001\ 646$ amu

total combined mass: 7.058 134 amu

mass defect

$= 7.058\ 134 \text{ amu} - 7.016\ 00 \text{ amu}$

$= 0.042\ 13$ amu

3. Given: measured atomic mass of $^6_3\text{Li} =$ 6.015 amu

Unknown: nuclear binding energy

3 protons: $(3 \times 1.007\ 276\ \text{amu})$

$= 3.021\ 828\ \text{amu}$

3 neutrons: $(3 \times 1.008\ 665\ \text{amu})$

$= 3.025\ 995\ \text{amu}$

3 electrons: $(3 \times 0.000\ 5486\ \text{amu})$

$= 0.001\ 646\ \text{amu}$

total combined mass: 6.049 469 amu

mass defect

$= 6.049\ 469\ \text{amu} - 6.015\ \text{amu}$

$= 0.034\ 469\ \text{amu}$

$= (0.034\ 469\ \text{amu})\left(\dfrac{1.6605 \times 10^{-27}\ \text{kg}}{1\ \text{amu}}\right)$

$= 5.7235 \times 10^{-29}\ \text{kg}$

$E = mc^2$

$= (5.7235 \times 10^{-29}\ \text{kg})(3.00 \times 10^8\ \text{m/s})^2$

$= 5.15 \times 10^{-12}\ \text{kg} \cdot \text{m}^2/\text{s}^2$

$= 5.2 \times 10^{-12}\ \text{J}$

4. Given: measured atomic mass of $^{35}_{19}\text{K} =$ 34.988 011 amu

Unknown: nuclear binding energy for the nucleus

19 protons: $(19 \times 1.007\ 276\ \text{amu})$

$= 19.138\ 244\ \text{amu}$

16 neutrons: $(16 \times 1.008\ 665\ \text{amu})$

$= 16.138\ 64\ \text{amu}$

19 electrons: $(19 \times 0.000\ 5486\ \text{amu})$

$= 0.010\ 4234\ \text{amu}$

total combined mass: 35.287 307 amu

mass defect

$= 35.287\ 307\ \text{amu} - 34.988\ 011\ \text{amu}$

$= 0.299\ 296\ \text{amu}$

$= (0.299\ 296\ \text{amu})\left(\dfrac{1.6605 \times 10^{-27}\ \text{kg}}{1\ \text{amu}}\right)$

$= 4.9698 \times 10^{-28}\ \text{kg}$

$E = mc^2$

$= (4.9698 \times 10^{-28}\ \text{kg})(3.00 \times 10^8\ \text{m/s})^2$

$= 4.47 \times 10^{-11}\ \text{kg} \cdot \text{m}^2/\text{s}^2$

$= 4.47 \times 10^{-11}\ \text{J}$

5. Given: measured atomic mass of $_{11}^{23}\text{Na}$ = 22.989 767 amu

Unknown: nuclear binding energy for the nucleus

11 protons: $(11 \times 1.007\ 276\ \text{amu})$

$= 11.080\ 036\ \text{amu}$

12 neutrons: $(12 \times 1.008\ 665\ \text{amu})$

$= 12.103\ 98\ \text{amu}$

11 electrons: $(11 \times 0.000\ 5486\ \text{amu})$

$= 0.006\ 0346\ \text{amu}$

total combined mass: 23.190 051 amu

mass defect

$= 23.190\ 051\ \text{amu} - 22.989\ 767\ \text{amu}$

$= 0.200\ 284\ \text{amu}$

$= (0.200\ 284\ \text{amu})\left(\dfrac{1.6605 \times 10^{-27}\ \text{kg}}{1\ \text{amu}} \right)$

$= 3.3257 \times 10^{-28}\ \text{kg}$

$E = mc^2$

$= (3.3257 \times 10^{-28}\ \text{kg})(3.00 \times 10^8\ \text{m/s})^2$

$= 2.99 \times 10^{-11}\ \text{kg} \cdot \text{m}^2/\text{s}^2$

$= 2.99 \times 10^{-11}\ \text{J}$

---

6. Given: nuclear binding energy of $_{19}^{35}\text{K}$ = $4.47 \times 10^{-11}\ \text{J}$

Unknown: binding energy per nucleon

$_{19}^{35}\text{K}\text{:}\ \left(\dfrac{4.47 \times 10^{-11}\ \text{J}}{35\ \text{nucleons}} \right)$

$= 1.28 \times 10^{-12}\ \text{J}$

---

7. Given: nuclear binding energy of $_{11}^{23}\text{Na}$ = $2.99 \times 10^{-11}\ \text{J}$

Unknown: binding energy per nucleon

$_{11}^{23}\text{Na}\text{:}\ \left(\dfrac{2.99 \times 10^{-11}\ \text{J}}{23\ \text{nucleons}} \right)$

$= 1.30 \times 10^{-12}\ \text{J}$

8. Given: measured atomic mass of $^{238}_{92}U$ = 238.050 784 amu

Unknown: binding energy per nucleon

92 protons: $(92 \times 1.007\ 276\ \text{amu})$

$= 92.669\ 392\ \text{amu}$

146 neutrons: $(146 \times 1.008\ 665\ \text{amu})$

$= 147.265\ 090\ \text{amu}$

92 electrons: $(92 \times 0.000\ 548\ 6\ \text{amu})$

$= 0.050\ 471\ 2\ \text{amu}$

total combined mass: 239.984 95 amu

mass defect

$= 239.984\ 95\ \text{amu} - 238.050\ 784\ \text{amu}$

$= 1.934\ 17\ \text{amu}$

$= (1.934\ 17\ \text{amu})\left(\dfrac{1.6605 \times 10^{-27}\ \text{kg}}{1\ \text{amu}} \right)$

$= 3.2117 \times 10^{-27}\ \text{kg}$

$E = mc^2$

$= (3.2117 \times 10^{-27}\ \text{kg})(3.00 \times 10^8\ \text{m/s})^2$

$= 2.891 \times 10^{-10}\ \text{kg} \cdot \text{m}^2/\text{s}^2$

$= 2.891 \times 10^{-10}\ \text{J}$

binding energy/nucleon

$= \left(\dfrac{2.891 \times 10^{-10}\ \text{J}}{238\ \text{nucleons}} \right)$

$= 1.21 \times 10^{-12}\ \text{J/nucleon}$

---

9. Given: nuclear binding energy of $^{56}_{26}Fe$ = 7.89×10^{-11} J

Unknown: amount of mass lost in kg

$E = mc^2$

$m = E/c^2$

$= \dfrac{7.89 \times 10^{-11}\ \text{J}}{(3.00 \times 10^8\ \text{m/s})^2}$

$= 8.77 \times 10^{-28}\ \text{kg}$

Solutions Manual *continued*

10. Given: measured atomic mass of deuterium = 2.0140 amu

Unknown: binding energy for 1 mole of deuterium atoms

deuterium = ^2_1H

1 proton: $(1 \times 1.007\ 276\ \text{amu})$

   = 1.007 276 amu

1 neutron: $(1 \times 1.008\ 665\ \text{amu})$

   = 1.008 665 amu

1 electron: $(1 \times 0.000\ 548\ 6\ \text{amu})$

   = 0.000 548 6 amu

total combined mass: 2.016 4896 amu

mass defect

= 2.016 4896 amu – 2.014 0 amu

= 0.002 489 6 amu

= $(0.002\ 489\ 6\ \text{amu})\left(\dfrac{1.6605 \times 10^{-27}\ \text{kg}}{1\ \text{amu}}\right)$

= 4.1339×10^{-30} kg

$E = mc^2$

   = $(4.1339 \times 10^{-30}\ \text{kg})(3.00 \times 10^8\ \text{m/s})^2$

   = $3.72 \times 10^{-13}\ \text{kg} \cdot \text{m}^2/\text{s}^2$

   = 3.72×10^{-13} J

binding energy per mol

= $(3.72 \times 10^{-13}$ J/atom)

$\times\ (6.022 \times 10^{23}$ atoms/mol)

= 2.24×10^{11} J/mol

---

11. Given: $^{43}_{19}K \longrightarrow\ ^{43}_{20}Ca\ +\ \underline{\quad ? \quad}$

Mass number: 43 – 43 = 0

atomic number: 19 – 20 = –1

? = $^0_{-1}e$

---

12. Given: $^{233}_{92}U \longrightarrow\ ^{229}_{90}Th\ +\ \underline{\quad ? \quad}$

mass number: 233 – 229 = 4

atomic number: 92 – 90 = 2

? = ^4_2He

---

13. Given: $^{11}_{6}C\ +\ \underline{\quad ? \quad} \longrightarrow\ ^{11}_{5}B$

mass number: 11 – 11 = 0

atomic number: 5 – 6 = –1

? = $^0_{-1}e$

Solutions Manual *continued*

14. Given: $^{13}_{7}\text{N} \longrightarrow {}^{0}_{+1}e + \underline{\quad ? \quad}$

mass number: $13 - 0 = 13$

atomic number: $7 - 1 = 6$

$? = {}^{13}_{6}\text{C}$

15. Given: $^{210}_{84}\text{Po}$

Unknown: the nuclear equation for the release of an alpha particle by $^{210}_{84}\text{Po}$

mass number: $210 - 4 = 206$ atomic number: $84 - 2 = 82$

$^{206}_{82}\text{Pb}$

$^{210}_{84}\text{Po} \longrightarrow {}^{4}_{2}\text{He} + {}^{206}_{82}\text{Pb}$

16. Given: $^{210}_{82}\text{Pb}$

Unknown: the nuclear equation for the release of a beta particle by $^{210}_{82}\text{Pb}$

Mass number: $210 - 0 = 210$

atomic number: $82 - (-1) = 83$

$\longrightarrow {}^{210}_{83}\text{Bi}$

$^{210}_{82}\text{Pb} \longrightarrow {}^{0}_{-1}\beta + {}^{210}_{83}\text{Bi}$

17. Given: $^{239}_{93}\text{Np} \longrightarrow {}^{0}_{-1}\beta + \underline{\quad ? \quad}$

mass number: $239 - 0 = 239$

atomic number : $93 - (-1) = 94$

$? = {}^{239}_{94}\text{Pu}$

18. Given: $^{9}_{4}\text{Be} + {}^{4}_{2}\text{He} \longrightarrow \underline{\quad ? \quad}$

mass number: $9 + 4 = 13$

atomic number: $4 + 2 = 6$

$? = {}^{13}_{6}\text{C}$

19. Given: $^{32}_{15}\text{P} + \underline{\quad ? \quad} \longrightarrow {}^{33}_{15}\text{P}$

mass number: $33 - 32 = 1$

atomic number: $15 - 15 = 0$

$? = {}^{1}_{0}n$

20. Given: $^{236}_{92}\text{U} \longrightarrow {}^{94}_{36}\text{Kr} + \underline{\quad ? \quad} + 3{}^{1}_{0}n$

mass number: $236 - 94 - 3 = 139$

atomic number: $92 - 36 - 0 = 56$

$? = {}^{139}_{56}\text{Ba}$

21. Given: original mass of radon-222 = 4.38 µg
half-life of radon-222 = 3.8 days
time elapsed = 15.2 days

Unknown: mass of radon-222 remaining

number of half-lives

$= (15.2 \text{ days})\left(\dfrac{1 \text{ half-life}}{3.8 \text{ days}}\right)$

$= 4$ half-lives

amount of radon-222 remaining

$= 4.38 \text{ µg} \times \left(\dfrac{1}{2}\right)^{4} = 0.274 \text{ µg}$

22. Given: half-life of uranium-238 = 4.46×10^9 years

Unknown: time needed for $\frac{7}{8}$ of sample to decay

amount of uranium-238 remaining

$= \frac{1}{8} = 0.125 = \left(\frac{1}{2}\right)^3$

$\longrightarrow = 3$ half-lives

time needed for decay

$= (4.46 \times 10^9 \text{ years})(3) = 1.34 \times 10^{10}$ years

23. Given: half-life of carbon-14 = 5715 years

Unknown: time needed for $\frac{1}{2}$ of sample to remain

time needed for decay for $\frac{1}{2}$ of sample to decay

$= 1$ half-life $= 5715$ years

24. Given: half-life of iodine-131 = 8.040 days

Unknown: percentage of a sample remaining after 40.2 days

number of half-lives

$= (40.2 \text{ days})\left(\frac{1 \text{ half-life}}{8.040 \text{ days}}\right) = 5$ half-lives

percent of sample remaining after 5 half-lives

$= \left(\frac{1}{2}\right)^5 \times 100 = 3.13\%$

25. Given: original mass of plutonium-239 = 100 g

half-life of plutonium-239 = 24110 years

time elapsed = 96440 years

Unknown: mass of plutonium-239 remaining

number of half-lives

$= (96440 \text{ years})\left(\frac{1 \text{ half-life}}{24110 \text{ years}}\right)$

$= 4$ half-lives

amount of plutonium-239 remaining after 4 half-lives

$= 100 \text{ g} \times \left(\frac{1}{2}\right)^4 = 6.25$ g

26. Given: half-life of thorium-227 = 18.72 days

Unknown: number of days needed for $\frac{3}{4}$ of a given amount to decay

amount remaining

$= \frac{1}{4} = 0.25 = \left(\frac{1}{2}\right)^2$

$\longrightarrow 2$ half-lives

length of time for decay

$= (18.72 \text{ days})(2) = 37.44$ days

27. Given: half-life of protactinium-234 = 6.69 hours

Unknown: fraction of a given amount remaining after 26.76 hours

number of half-lives

$= (26.76 \text{ hours})\left(\frac{1 \text{ half-life}}{6.69 \text{ hours}}\right) = 4$ half-lives

amount remaining after 4 half-lives

$= \left(\frac{1}{2}\right)^4 = \frac{1}{16}$

28. Given: original mass of radium-226 = 15 mg

half-life of radium-226 = 1599 years

time elapsed = 6396 years

Unknown: mass of radium-226 remaining

number of half-lives

$$= (6396 \text{ years}) \left(\frac{1 \text{ half-life}}{1599 \text{ years}} \right)$$

$$= 4 \text{ half-lives}$$

amount remaining

$$= 15 \text{ mg} \times \left(\frac{1}{2} \right)^4$$

$$= 0.94 \text{ mg}$$

29. Given: original mass of radium-226 = 0.25 g

half-life of radium-226 = 1599 years

time elapsed = 4797 years

Unknown: mass of radium-226 remaining

number of half-lives

$$= (4797 \text{ years}) \left(\frac{1 \text{ half-life}}{1599 \text{ years}} \right)$$

$$= 3 \text{ half-lives amount remaining}$$

$$= 0.25 \text{ g} \times \left(\frac{1}{2} \right)^3$$

$$= 0.03125 \text{ g}$$

30. Given: half-life of radium-224 = 3.66 days

time elapsed = 7.32 days

mass remaining of radium-224 = 0.05 g

Unknown: original mass of radium-224

number of half-lives

$$= (7.32 \text{ days}) \left(\frac{1 \text{ half-life}}{3.66 \text{ days}} \right)$$

$$= 2 \text{ half-lives}$$

$x =$ original amount

$$(x) \left(\frac{1}{2} \right)^2 = 0.05 \text{ g}$$

$$x = (0.05 \text{ g}) \times \left(\frac{2}{1} \right)^2 = 0.2 \text{ g}$$